Diary of a Language Teacher

The European Language Classroom

Diary of a Language Teacher

Joachim Appel

Heinemann English Language Teaching
A division of Heinemann Publishers (Oxford) Ltd
Halley Court, Jordan Hill, Oxford OX2 8EJ

OXFORD MADRID ATHENS PARIS FLORENCE
PRAGUE SÃO PAULO CHICAGO MELBOURNE AUCKLAND
SINGAPORE TOKYO IBADAN GABORONE JOHANNESBURG
PORTSMOUTH (NH)

ISBN 0 435 24076 5

Series design by Mike Brain
Cover photo by Moggy

Printed and bound in Great Britain by The Bath Press

Acknowledgements

DIARY WRITING is a lonely pastime. Producing a book is a co-operative effort. I would never have thought how co-operative it is. I could not have completed this book without lots of help from others. Mario Rinvolucri first encouraged me to embark on a project of this kind. Siegfried Ley, who unfortunately did not live to see this project finished, provided me with advice both as my teacher at secondary school and 20 years on. Early and late versions of the manuscript were read and commented on by Peter Auer, Wolfgang Frank, Cristina and Wolfgang Schlegelmilch and Peter Siegle, as well as three anonymous readers. Debbie Wilson provided much needed typing and Jenny Gibb much needed storage. Sometimes institutions can become as familiar as persons. For me the National Library of Scotland in Edinburgh and the University Library of Konstanz have been such places for many years. I would like to thank both the institutions and the people who run them. Finally, I wish to thank those who made this book happen: my editors Arthur van Essen and Jill Florent, the staff at Heinemann and Louise Elkins: for their help, their encouragement and their stamina in working on the non-native output of a non-native author.

To Cristina

Contents

The author and series editor

Joachim Appel was born in 1953 and grew up in the south of Germany. Since 1974 he has divided his time between Germany and Britain. After a first degree in German and English at Konstanz University he went on to do an MSc in Applied Linguistics at Edinburgh University. He has accumulated several years' work experience as a teacher of German at British universities and as a house husband in Scotland, where his first son was born. In Germany he spent eight years as a secondary school teacher. He has published a number of articles about teaching languages in schools. At the moment he is living with his wife and three children in rural surroundings, commuting to Munich University where he is on secondment to teach teachers.

Arthur van Essen MA PhD, is professor of Applied Linguistics at the University of Groningen in the Netherlands. He has been involved in EFL for the past 35 years as a teacher, a teacher trainer, and a writer of coursebooks. He has published widely and has lectured both in the UK and continental Europe. He was Vice-Chair of the International Association of Teachers of English as a Foreign Language (IATEFL) in the 1980s and the first elected Chair of Networking English Language Learning in Europe (NELLE). He is currently the Head of the Department of Language and Communication at the University of Groningen.

The European Language Classroom

EUROPEAN FOREIGN-LANGUAGE CLASSROOMS share a long tradition of language teaching and language learning. Most European nations are close to each other or they are bi- or multilingual themselves. The need to communicate with one another across languages is therefore an old and obvious one. Business is conducted in many European languages, and many Europeans spend their holidays in a neighbouring European country. Learning and teaching foreign languages is of enormous importance for Europe.

Traditionally, European foreign-language teachers share their learners' native language and culture. They have themselves been through the process of learning another language. As a result, they are themselves at least bilingual, but more often than not, multilingual. Such teachers tap a vast resource of both personal and collective experience. This is what sets the European language classroom apart from other language classrooms, whether native or second.

The European Language Classroom Series addresses issues that concern foreign-language teachers in both public and private-sector education. It aims to help you, the teacher or teacher trainer, to bridge the gap between current language teaching and learning theory and classroom practice, and to share and benefit from the expertise of foreign-language teachers who speak their pupils' mother tongue.

Individual titles in the series focus on: problems facing the novice teacher; developing classroom skills; intercultural learning and teaching; project learning; teaching a foreign language across the curriculum in state schools; managing change in teacher-training programmes; language for specific purposes; the psychology of foreign-language teaching; etc. In view of the rapid developments taking place in Europe the series is open-ended.

The authors share these concerns and have joined the team on the strength of the contribution they have made to foreign-language education, either in their own country or at European level. Authors will call on their readers to share their often considerable experience as teachers of at least one (and sometimes more than one) foreign language, and as learners of usually more than one foreign language.

Meeting the challenges posed by foreign-language teaching in a Europe in which all the barriers are lifted is what the European Language Classroom is about.

Prologue: School

I HAVE ALWAYS HAD mixed feelings about school: plain fear when I was twelve, the sweet taste of insurrection when I was sixteen, and blasé fatigue before I left. If I was to go back as a teacher, I promised myself at the time, it would be to change things or at least to avoid mistakes. I wanted to be well prepared for the job. So I eagerly plunged into books about methodology. When reading those books I had a nagging vision of classes running riot, but the further I got into my studies the more remote school became. I kept postponing my entry into the school system and was looking around for alternatives. Teaching, yes, but preferably under more humane circumstances. I went abroad, did a degree in Applied Linguistics and taught conversation classes. Yet at the back of my mind I kept asking myself: would I survive at school? I turned to friends who had gone into school teaching. Some moaned how hard it was out there in 'real life'. Others said it was a matter of trying it out. This I did.

School put me firmly in my place. I found myself at the very bottom of a hierarchy. Instead of indulging in academic small talk at the coffee bar, I was waiting for gaps in my supervisor's conversation during morning break, trying to get in a question about my next teaching project.

Classes knew I depended on their co-operation for the exams I had to take to become a teacher. They left me in no doubt about it. On the other hand they gave me the occasional – very useful – hint about teaching. 'Don't revise too much. Carry out your threats. Only threaten to do what you can carry out.' Discipline was not the problem, at least not initially. It was kept at bay by an experienced teacher who sat at the back of the classroom. Once he had to leave before the end of the lesson. It was as if he had pulled the plug.

With all my experience and additional qualifications, including an MA thesis on the role of questions in language teaching, I felt well qualified. Once on the job, it all counted for very little. My university education had taught me to recognize structures in sentences, novels and discourse. The children wanted stories. I thought I could teach, but school teaching, it seemed, was a whole new craft to learn. Lessons had to be much more carefully stage-managed. I used to consider it the hallmark of a good conversation lesson if it went on beyond the time at which it was supposed to finish. Now I found myself wrestling with minutes and even seconds in order to set the class homework before the bell went and the students with it. I was no longer analysing the role of questions. I had to ask the right ones. But how?

The English spoken by the teachers I was watching wasn't always perfect. However, it worked. It got their point across. I went to them with my lesson plans and checked the details. They told me how to say it in such a way that I would get an answer. I came up with questions like 'Could you give me the exact wording of what John says?' They narrowed it down to 'What were his words?' Teaching a class at the time seemed very much like working an unknown machine. You pulled the right levers and it did what you wanted it to do. I never knew what went on inside. How could I understand it and make it work?

I went back to where I had come from: the university library. I spent a few free evenings there looking for books that could help with my problems. Sure enough there were studies on language learning in schools and on methodology. Such studies were highly critical of school in general and language teaching in particular. Some of them read as if they had some secret axe to grind with the school-teaching profession. I read up on classroom interaction. The studies proved I had got it all wrong. As one friend said after his MA in Applied Linguistics: 'You go back to doing the wrong thing, but at least you know *why* it's wrong.' Seen from school, research seemed to belong to a different world. In this world, time was no object. What I was trying to read in my spare time was either long or complicated or both. In order to understand it you had to get through lots of jargon and technical apparatus, be it descriptive categories, statistics or flow-charts. In comparison, the practical recommendations at the end of such books seemed to amount to very little. Most often their statements were of a rather general nature, recommending more communication, more games, less teacher control – all of which I would gladly have subscribed to 300 pages earlier.

Everyday life at school was not about research. Research is controlling the variables; teaching is being controlled by them. At my workplace no factors could be isolated. On the contrary, they were hopelessly muddled. Research was about keeping things separate. Life meant everything at once. Research was about being pure. Life was about being eclectic. Research was about being rigorous and consistent. Life was about survival by any available means.

Luckily some of my new colleagues gave me hints about surviving, above all about surviving teaching exams. One colleague showed me how to teach grammar lessons entirely in English. It required a lot of planning and took me hours to work out. The class co-operated in my lessons because my supervising teacher had very tight control over it. The day came and I did my demonstration lesson on 'forms for the future'. I pushed the start button and while the lesson unfolded I more or less stood in front watching myself teaching and felt completely out of touch with the class. The lesson ended up being highly commended for its systematic approach, clear structure and the colourful blackboard diagrams.

After initial successes my performance as a teacher began to deteriorate. With all the supervision I was getting, plus my impending exams, I became more and more self-conscious. In the final phase of our training we were given a class to teach on our own and discipline very quickly got out of hand. My final marks were not bad, but I was criticized for not being strict enough. In the middle of the summer vacation, after I had given up hope of a teaching post and had started to pack all my school books into a cardboard box, I got a phone call offering me an interview. Four weeks later I took up employment as a teacher.

Introduction

WORK ON THIS BOOK started out from diaries I wrote as a teacher at a state secondary school over a period of six years. They are personal diaries rather than a professional record. I wrote them the night before lessons and during the lunch break after lessons. I wrote them in between and sometimes even during lessons, when the class was doing a written task. I wrote them in cafés, on trains and while waiting for trains. What they contain are not systematic observations, but subjective perceptions and impressions of everyday life at school – in short: experience. It was at the end of my first six years in school teaching that I turned to the pile of notebooks that had accumulated over the years, reread them and wondered if they could become a book on language-teaching practice. I had my doubts. Diaries are a risky genre to write. They are subjective, biased and always risk being vain. Their author is caught at a moment in time and lacks detachment. The outcome of what is described is open and there is no hindsight. Once written down, all those false impressions and misjudgements are there to stay. Moreover, diaries are a risky genre to publish, because it is an open question whether the worries and joys of the diary writer are really relevant to others. So what insights are there to be gained, especially for colleagues, from the 'inside view' this diary of a language teacher gives?[1] I think there can be two. The first is a view of the complexities of school practice. The second is a picture of individual development and change.

A view of the complexities of school practice

Publications on language teaching have often seen teaching practice as the lowest step of a staircase. At the top there is theory. Seen from the top, the staircase makes sense. Start out from theory, prove it through research, translate the findings into a syllabus, translate the syllabus into procedures and materials, translate these into teaching. My book tries to take a view from below. It was the view I had during these six years. This probably sounds as if I am trying to get my own back. I have tried not to – although there has been the odd temptation. What I have tried to do is to put practice first. My belief in this principle has been strengthened by more than my own personal experience.

In his book *The Reflective Practitioner,* Schön (1983) describes how the glamour of professionals in our society has faded over the last two decades, because 'experts' are no longer seen as providing relevant answers to the world's problems. One reason Schön pinpoints for this alleged failure is the way in which the 'professions' (be they medicine, architecture, management, law or teaching) have defined the relationship between their academic source disciplines and practice as one 'in which rigorous professional practitioners are instrumental problem solvers who select technical means best suited to particular purposes. Rigorous professional practitioners solve well-formed instrumental problems by applying theory and technique derived from systematic, preferably scientific knowledge' (Schön 1987

---

1 Teachers' diaries have recently attracted considerable research interest (cf McDonough 1994). Such studies mainly use diaries as a device for training teachers.

pp3–4). I had a glimpse of this relationship when I went back to the library during my first year in teaching. More recently, however, there has been an increased interest in 'turning the problem upside down' (Schön 1987 p12) by looking at the way practitioners address, reflect on and solve problems arising in professional practice. Schon has described various professionals, such as architects, psychotherapists, managers and teachers. Within educational research there have been studies of how individual teachers work and what the values and principles guiding their practice are (eg Elbaz 1983).

Reading these studies has strengthened me in my belief in the principle 'practice and experience first'. This principle has determined the shape and format of the seven chapters to follow. The first ('diary') part of each chapter consists of a number of episodes. For ease of reference and to indicate the significance of the episode, the entries have been given titles, usually a quotation from the text to follow. The second ('analysis') part of each chapter tries to explore and interpret the experience narrated in the episodes in the light of research findings. The episodes do not, of course, represent 'pure' experience assembled without any prior knowledge of theory. Neither the original diary entries nor even less their presentation in this book represent 'naïve' experience, collected on an 'empty slate'. (Nor are they, for reasons of confidentiality, entirely factual.) Putting together this book was a two-way process. I was sifting my personal and subjective evidence with certain guiding questions and concepts at the back of my mind. At the same time the concepts themselves were sifted and modified as they were confronted with the evidence.

One of the things to emerge when I tried to explore the reality of my own classroom was that the scope of the research I had to turn to was considerably wider than that on language teaching, because teaching the language was only one of my many concerns when I entered a classroom. There is usually a neat divide between different disciplines like methodology, education, psychology, etc. In the classroom, however, they occur quite inseparably, because they are all part of one person's practice. For this book this meant I had to leave the realm of English as a foreign language and look at studies on the sociology of the teaching profession, teacher health, the psychology of education, humanistic psychology, analysis of classroom interaction and classroom management. Needless to say that I have been both subjective and selective in choosing my sources. The picture I hope to present as a result is holistic in tendency. It tries to put language teaching into a wider educational perspective. I therefore write about education as much as about language teaching. As far as teaching children is concerned, both are, in my opinion, mutually dependent.

Educational questions, especially the relationship between students and teachers, are foundations for the teaching of any subject. Language teaching at school must therefore be considered in conjunction with them. If personal relations in the classroom are not healthy, teaching quickly becomes an empty ritual because there is no chance of it being effective in classes that are unruly, apathetic or hostile. Conversely, every method or piece of material a teacher uses has an educational impact. A change of seating arrangements means more than just changing the positions of chairs and tables. Teaching school children is more than the attainment of language objectives. I was often under the impression that language instruction in the school classroom was merely the stage on which the actual drama of education took place. One outcome of this drama has been described by the term 'hidden curriculum'.

It means that what children are taught at school is not so much the subject matter, ie the language, but rather attitudes and values, often controversial ones like obedience and discipline. A well-structured lesson may teach the 'Declaration of Independence' or the 'use of gerunds after prepositions' quite effectively. It may look good to an observer. At the same time the actual message it conveys to students is that only what the teacher says matters. As one school leaver wrote about the language lessons he had taken part in: 'I didn't bother to say anything in Mr B's lesson, because it was only his views that counted.'

All this, I believe, need not be so. Our hidden agenda need not be about imposing our will on classes, at least not exclusively. If there is educational significance to everything a teacher does, this significance can be negative as well as positive. I found, for instance, that changing what on the surface looked like almost irrelevant details (a gesture, a reaction, a tone of voice, a word chosen as an example) did affect the overall picture of what I was doing and that positive details had a cumulative effect, sometimes resulting in a change for the better. The second emphasis of this book is on such change.

Individual development and change

An emphasis on change does not necessarily combine well with one on practice. The practising teacher's resistance to educational change has often been the subject of complaint. Why is it that school practice has been going on as if advances in research had never happened? Elbaz, having worked in curriculum development in the seventies, found that teachers 'resent, and resist, efforts to change them' (Elbaz 1983 p 3). She also found one of the reasons for this. (Others will be looked at in Chapter 1.) It was that curriculum development left the teacher with very little autonomy, and indeed with the rather limited role of implementor:

> The teacher could at best be a facilitator, someone who had taken the trouble to understand the approach of the developer, to adapt it minimally to her own situation and to convey it faithfully to students. (Elbaz 1983 p 3)

Clark, investigating curriculum renewal in foreign language teaching, comes to a similar conclusion:

> The teacher's task is reduced to that of bringing about certain prespecified behavioural changes in all pupils in a predetermined stereotypical manner. Neither teachers nor pupils are considered as individuals with the need to teach and learn in mutually responsive ways towards ends that they themselves have agreed upon. (Clark 1987 p 34)

The staircase mentioned earlier not only symbolizes logical deduction. It also stands for a social hierarchy. It is hardly surprising that when changes are passed down this hierarchy, with policy makers being at the top and teachers being at the bottom end of the 'implementational staircase' (Reynolds and Saunders 1987 p 211), such changes do not translate into practical action in a straightforward and easy fashion. Reynolds and Saunders (1987) describe the difficulties of communication between people involved in change at different levels of the educational hierarchy and note as one principal problem that 'colleagues at the next step down [*sic*!] in the implementational staircase are more concerned to pick up justificatory vocabularies than to analyse the planning and implementation skills that they need.' (Reynolds and Saunders 1987 p211). Put more crudely, the maxim of practitioners (indeed a maxim I have heard more than once) in the face of change coming 'from above' is: 'Keep on doing the same thing but use the new name for it.' 'Justificatory vocabularies' in the field of language teaching abound. To take but one example, talking of 'functions' can cover a great variety of objectives in language teaching, from 'making a polite request' via 'describing completed actions' to 'verbalizing joy about a successful trick'. This means it is possible to have almost any objective (ie introducing a speech act, the present perfect or a textbook anecdote) covered by a terminology that is acceptable in terms of the 'current trend'. What changes is the terminology rather than what happens in the classroom.

The second emphasis of this book is therefore on change at an individual level. In describing it I am going to take the term 'teacher development' quite literally and look at my own development as a language teacher. How did I change, adapt, persist, advance or regress under the influence of my work situation? In presenting my 'findings' I have tried to bring together a narrative and a systematic reflection, autobiography and research, personal development and innovation in the field. How these combine in one person is, I believe, of some general interest, because any innovation that becomes effective in education is in some way bound up with teachers' and students' biographies. For instance, the particular stage at which a new idea reaches a teacher in his/her development may well decide whether this idea will be effective. To give an empirical example of the interplay between personal development and innovation: there is evidence in research literature (cf Rutter 1979) that open forms of teaching have a greater chance of success when used by an experienced teacher who can fall back on a routine if more experimental forms should fail. At the same time it is the inexperienced teacher who is more likely to innovate – for the very reason that he/she has not established a routine yet. However, innovation in the early stages of a teaching career often adds to insecurity, and attempts at it can be fraught and abandoned too early.

In trying to plot my development as a teacher I have decided to give this book the shape of a chronology, which, of course, does not represent the exact sequence of events but which, I hope, sufficiently captures its strands and turning points. The three main parts to this book are:

Part One: *Survival*
Part Two: *Change*
Part Three: *Routine*

Part One: *Survival* describes the difficulties I encountered when I started in my first teaching post, discipline being the most prominent one among them.

Chapter 1: *Teachers' work* looks at some of the strains of teaching and the reasons behind them. It looks at studies of the teacher's 'workplace'. The importance of classroom control and the uncertainty of the teaching situation as well as staffroom relations are discussed as important factors affecting innovation in schools. The chapter goes on to explore possible links between classroom control and alienation of students from what they are supposed to learn.

Many of the difficulties described in Chapter 1 call for long-term rather than short-term solutions. However, teachers (and especially beginning teachers) have to deal with many situations that call for immediate action. Chapter 2, *Coping with discipline*, therefore offers a 'first-aid kit', ie a personal selection of measures and strategies for survival in the face of adversity. These include aspects like first encounters between the teacher and a class, constancy of the teacher's measures, the creation of 'breathing spaces' for the teacher during lessons and, finally, flexibility and humour.

Part Two: *Change* is no longer exclusively about coping with the classroom situation, but about influencing it as well. It describes what were, for me, new perceptions as well as new methods.

Chapter 3: *A different angle: humanism* starts out from a number of (for me at the time) surprising perceptions in the classroom which opened up new insights into how students worked and how I could do more than survive as a teacher. These windows had almost exclusively to do with interpersonal relations in the classroom. My analysis uses concepts from humanistic psychology (Rogers' well-known 'empathy', 'valuing', 'realness' as well as learner autonomy) to elucidate why certain courses of action so unexpectedly turned out to be successful. It makes suggestions as to how these concepts can become reality in the language classroom.

Chapter 4: *Depth* reports my attempt to introduce new teaching methods. These were learner-centred or 'humanistic' exercises (in my case those suggested by Maley and Duff 1978, Moskowitz 1978, Morgan and Rinvolucri 1983, Frank and Rinvolucri 1983). The chapter starts out from the concept of 'depth' (Stevick 1976) which was chosen to capture the personal relevance that the foreign language and the way it is taught has for students. It examines the communicative approach to language teaching and humanistic exercises in the light of this concept. Finally, it takes a detailed look at student feedback on how the exercises had worked for them. Students' social needs as well as their need for autonomy and security, together with their quest for reality are the topics of this analysis.

Part Three: *Routine* looks at what role the changes described in Part Two can play in day-to-day teaching. It shows how humanistic principles can enhance routine work.

Chapter 5: *Relevant reading – relevant writing* investigates two areas of language teaching: the teaching of literature and the teaching of writing. It describes the contribution humanistic principles can make to these.

Chapter 6: *Can exams be humane?* tries to suggest how the sufferings of both examiners and examinees can be reduced.

Chapter 7: *A routine lesson* describes a number of procedures (rituals, greetings, bilingual exercises, adaptations of 'alternative methods'). It looks at how these can make a lesson, especially its beginning phase, controllable for the teacher and at the same time open to student contributions.

This book is written for both experienced and beginning teachers. Beginning teachers, I assumed, would be interested in suggestions and advice. I have tried to supply some about discipline (Chapter 2). This is followed by practical sections in Chapter 3. Chapters 5 to 7 are centred entirely around practical problems and solutions. In the concluding chapter I turn to some of the problems experienced teachers might face. I do so by investigating the meaning that routine and experience have for me after the six years of teaching that are now about to unfold.

Part One
Survival

Chapter 1 **Teachers' work**

Diary

....

7th August

Stage fright

'When I start waking up during the night, I know it's the end of the vacation,' Arthur told me over a beer. He has just finished his second year as a teacher. I thought there would be an end to stage fright after the teaching exams were over. School starts on Monday. Tomorrow at ten I am seeing the headmaster.

8th August

Don't try to be their friend

The crunch, the head told me, is grade 10. Grade 5 should be OK. Everybody is keen to have them, because at the age of ten or eleven they are still kids and enthusiastic. They are supposed to be good fun to teach. With grade 10 it is different. They are 16 and in the midst of adolescence. 'Adolescence', he said, 'is a long dark tunnel.' Many pupils of the class I am to take will leave school at the end of the year. I will have only limited influence over them. 'Don't try to be their friend,' he added, 'they don't want that. They want a teacher, someone they respect.'

16th August

We all go to the window

First lesson in grade 5. It went fine. I told them to wait at the door until I (teachers are the people with keys) had unlocked it. They went in quietly. I talked to them for a while, until they started looking out of the window. I could under-stand that, because the school is high up on a hill and the view was, on this summer day, magnificent. I suggested we all go to the window and have a look round. I asked them to show me their villages in the distance. They hesitantly did so. I could see it was not their idea of a first lesson in secondary school.

1

19th August

A new pupil

First lesson in grade 10. What a difference! They burst out laughing when they saw me. They thought I was a new pupil. I didn't stand a chance. Their boisterous welcome had intimidated me. I couldn't hide it. I had gone in with pretty low expectations anyway. They are timetabled for three lessons a week, one at the end of the afternoon after a PE lesson, one just before lunch, one very early in the morning. I felt I had to be open with them and started the lesson by acknowledging that it would be a difficult year for all of us.

31st August

As long as it isn't grammar

They say they hate grammar. Anything, as long as it isn't grammar. One of them, Eric, came to me at the end of the lesson and asked why you can't say 'he doesn't writes'. I took a deep breath. It's their sixth year of English and both the syllabus and the book assume that students can take part in discussions on the energy crisis using infinitive constructions. The class does not know about infinitives. Nor do they want to know. It's grammar. Funnily enough they can be very persistent when there is something they don't understand, but you can never predict when this will happen. I usually try to explain, but of course there is never enough time, because I have to rush on to the next class. When I saw them again today I put the form 'he doesn't write' on the blackboard, but Eric seemed to have forgotten his question. In any case, he no longer showed interest in the answer. Instead, someone else challenged me (who is the one being tested?) on 'They did not expect John to find a solution'. 'Why "to"?' I managed to explain. It seemed to make a difference for the rest of the lesson.

13th September

Missed the vital clue

Four weeks into the school year. 10a has developed into a nightmare. I don't know how it happened. I lost control. I didn't even notice that it happened. I am on the defensive. I must have missed the vital clue. Acknowledging their difficulties might have been a mistake. Trying to solve their grammar problems for them was probably another. The rule of the game now is that their English and their learning are my responsibility instead of theirs.

14th September

Tunnel vision

Staying rational when I write about an incident is one thing, being in the acoustic, organizational and emotional turmoil of the classroom is another. Far too often I am caught up in chaos. I watch myself going into the classroom armed with the right plans and doing the wrong thing. 'Adolescence is a long dark tunnel.' So are my lessons. Looking at them is like looking through a tunnel, too. The only thing I can see at its end is a tiny segment of reality. This segment is 10a. I cannot help looking at it. I now measure my professional success in terms of success in 10a. I keep telling myself: most lessons, especially those in grade 5, are going well. Yet this does not seem to count. What counts is 10a and whether I survive them three times a week. If things go well in 10a, everything is good. Thursday 12.45 and I am finished with them for the week. It feels as if the weekend has already started. Fridays and Saturdays are good days, because I can allow myself not to think of them. Come Sunday afternoon it starts all over again.

15th September

Oliver

The spot I can't look away from is Oliver. He constantly disturbs my lessons and drains me of all my energy. Oliver is choleric by nature. Handing back a test to someone seems, in theory, to be a straightforward task. Not with Oliver. When he doesn't like his grade – and usually he doesn't – he scrunches up the paper, takes his textbook and hammers on the table with it. When I gave back their word test yesterday, he put his head on the table and kept drumming on it with his fists.

5th October

Short-termism

What would teaching be without coffee? Today someone forgot to switch on the coffee machine. I could hardly work up enough energy to face the next class after the break. Although teaching should be about long-term objectives ('learning for life'), my work is governed by short-termism. Get into top gear for the beginning of the lesson, get the show started, shout a couple of times, relax when they have started the task. More coffee during the next break. It can't be healthy. It continues like this in the afternoons and evenings. Postpone preparing classes. Tonight it is marking the word test that should have been given back ages ago. Having finally marked it, I realize it is too late to do any planning that goes beyond tomorrow's lesson. And I'm too tired even for that. So I grab the book and, at the last possible minute, think up something that will fill tomorrow's time slots. It is indeed difficult to keep anything long-term in view. There is always something urgent.

10th October

Little skirmishes at the beginning

One of my daily skirmishes. I go into the classroom. Jessica is aiming a spray can at her neighbour. It is hair spray. The boys in the last row of seats pull their shirts over their noses. They say they cannot breathe. Michael is coming in late, or rather he is being kicked in by Jens. I stand in front of the blackboard. My arms are crossed behind my back. The handle for moving the blackboard up and down is my only anchor. I resist the impulse to shout. It is bad for the voice which I need for the rest of the day. I wait. The pit of my stomach feels tense. (I have recently had stomach trouble, too much coffee probably.) My head is empty. Desperation creeps in. I am still waiting. We were taught never to try and speak louder than the class. They say it is better to wait until the class has calmed down.

Last week I couldn't bear waiting any longer and walked out on them spending five nerve-wracking minutes in the staffroom until, finally, a group of them came and asked me to come back. They were quiet for the rest of the lesson. It won't work twice though. Today I shout. They calm down. The lesson can begin. At that moment the door is flung open and in comes Oliver. He is late back from break. There are shouts from the class. 'What have you been up to?' It is like having, with immense effort, piled up a tower of bricks and now the pile is toppled. Toppled by Oliver. I challenge him. But Oliver always has good reasons. He sits down talking to his neighbour. I explode. He almost seems to have waited for this as an opportunity to take the stage and have one of his little showdowns with me. I fall for it. Like so often. I yell. He yells, protesting that others have been talking to their neighbours as well. In the end I send him out. The lesson proceeds peacefully over the next five minutes. I ask Oliver back in. He stays quiet. I write a lot on the blackboard, my back turned to the class. Unrest starts again. I have forgotten to tell them to copy it. I tell them to now. The noise gets less. I look at my lesson plan. I have only covered two out of five points from my programme. I tell them to hurry up with the copying. They don't. I have got five minutes left for the next exercises, which I have to get finished because the homework I want them to do is based on it. I start explaining. We do one sentence. They don't understand. I explain again. My explanations are interrupted by the bell. I have been too busy explaining to look at my watch. I try to tell them what their homework is, but they have already started packing up. I shout – at the top of my voice – page number and number of the exercise. I write them on the blackboard to be safe, but the first ones are already leaving the room.

1st November

Forms for the future

Sunday night again. This week it's the future tense. For once I have got the material sorted out because I have done a (successful!) teaching exam on it. I have drawn out my treasured grammar lesson that once earned me a reputation during training: 'forms for the future'. An inductive grammar lesson, completely in the target language. It starts from a well-constructed text containing all the relevant forms and then leads, in a smooth step-by-step transition, up to the difference between 'I will go'/'I am going to go'/'I am going'/'I will be going'.

2nd November

Fell flat on its face

Treasured grammar lesson fell flat on its face. Two years ago when I taught it as a demonstration lesson, with my tutor sitting at the back and the class nicely subdued, I actually managed to get through the programme in one 45-minute lesson. Today I only got through a fraction of it. I suddenly became aware of how much time all the little exchanges and exhortations, the half minutes and quarter minutes when I wait for them to calm down, add up to. Not to mention all the time I spent answering questions.

3rd November

Unbearable perfection

Talked to a grey and experienced colleague about my demonstration lesson and how it had gone wrong. Served me right, he said. No class could cope with ideally planned lessons more often than once every couple of weeks. The degree of concentration necessary for such ideal lessons is beyond the kids, in fact beyond anybody.

10th January

But what would a visitor see?

Headmaster told me that he and the deputy would come round 'during the next few weeks to have a look at how you are getting on'. I went into the next lesson in sheer panic. I suddenly looked at grade 5 with the eyes of my superiors. I watched myself setting the class some written work which would last them through the better part of the lesson and would give me some much-needed time to catch my breath before I had to confront 10a again in the next lesson. Good. But what would a visitor see? What impression would the head and his deputy get? Surely the emphasis in 'having a look at how you are getting on' lay on how I was getting on, ie not on how the class learnt but on how I, the teacher, taught.

12th January

Commiserating

Friendly hints are being dropped by commiserating colleagues (the story of the impending visit is spreading fast): 'He doesn't like it when you sit on the table. Above all, it's got to be quiet.' I am trying to oblige. I have started treating some of the lessons as dress rehearsals for the event. My lessons become very tense.

20th January

Flu

Down with the flu for a week. I call it the flu, in any case. Half the class were sniffing. On Thursday my voice started to go. I could feel it getting deeper from lesson to lesson. Went in on Friday for the first two lessons because they were writing a test and finding another date is worse than illness. Went home after that. Tried to do some marking over the weekend, but felt too exhausted to get beyond the first couple of test books. On Monday I simply could not face going back to school.

3rd February

Two lesson plans

It's a week since I got back. Still waiting for their visit. I have gone over to operating two lesson plans. One in case I am on my own, the other in the event of a visit. The first is a no-witness and therefore no-frills version in which I simply get on with whatever we are doing. The other one is more polished, with a blackboard diagram, question–answer sequences and a coda to round off the topic.

8th February

The visit

The visit took place today. Lesson went smoothly. The kids were extraordinarily well behaved. I got through the material quicker than I thought and had to think up an additional activity. In the 'post-mortem' my visitors turned out to be much more sensible than the gossip that I had been told about them had led me to believe.

2nd March

Solid everyday work

Staff meeting. Head read out a letter from the inspectorate which sounded like an ironic illustration of last month's tribulations: in a letter to all staff a senior adviser was telling us quite passionately (a rare document) not to concentrate so much on individual 'show' lessons when he was coming to visit. This was not what he would like to see. He would much rather have routine lessons, solid everyday work that showed long-term effects. The problem is that our professional assessment and with it promotion rests on the inspection of individual lessons that are supposed to be excellent.

16th March

Closed doors

One good thing during training was that I could sit in on other teachers' classes. Today I would benefit from an occasional visit to a colleague. It would help to put into perspective what the others in the staffroom say. But teachers work behind closed doors. The privacy of the classroom is sacred. Unless someone comes on an inspection, of course.

18th March

Breaking the privacy rule

K (we started at the school together) is breaking the privacy rule. He comes back into the staffroom after a lesson telling the others how difficult it has been to calm down the class. One of my colleagues tells me he thinks K is a fool to do this. It would destroy his reputation, if he had any left to destroy. None of those K was opening up to would try to help him. In fact, even if they did, there wouldn't be much they could do for him, because in the end it was a matter between him and the class.

4th April

No youth is worse

Staffroom talk: no youth is worse than today's youth. The others never stop complaining about children's lack of concentration, lack of work ethic, etc. No mention of how much the world has changed. The hours spent in front of video screens and computer games. As a lead-in to the lesson I regularly ask students 'What did you do yesterday?' 'I played with my computer' is what more than half the class says regularly. In trying to make lessons 'interesting' school has entered a futile race with the entertainment industry. More videos. More coloured photographs. Yet when I ask pupils about school, they are still bored. Or is it only their tolerance for boredom that has gone down? In any case, we can't win.

5th April

Community of moaners

Staffroom talk part two. It is brimming over with anger and aggression. It is a release of tension, it is irrational and it accentuates the negative (red ink mentality). Come and join the community of moaners. I do, too. I need it. But the unity is deceptive because its sense of shared suffering is easily mistaken for a set of shared values, which, of course, does not exist. In a staff of about 100 there is, in fact, very little consensus on anything. There is a school policy which helps, but it does not go beyond a bare minimum of general disciplinary rules. When individual cases are up for discussion (like G, who continually misses lessons) there is, 'for time reasons', hardly any discussion about the actual case, but only about its formalities. At best, disciplinary 'measures' are agreed on. Everyone is happy when the meeting is over and nobody had to lay open his/her classroom practice. The possibility that difficulties with a child could actually be difficulties between the child and the teacher, ie a problem of personal relations, seems taboo.

Staffroom talk is infectious. Often it is just a remark, dropped at the wrong moment, that sticks. Today, for instance, I got 'infected' by one of these stories. The colleague teaching Latin said how dismally bad 10a was, how he had come down hard and how it had worked. I am the next one to go into the class to teach them, my ears still ringing with the colleague's remarks. I reckon I have to take preventive measures too. This turns out to be the wrong line altogether, because either the class has calmed down now or my colleague's perceptions were wrong. In any case, they do not understand why I am suddenly so strict. It takes half the lesson to get the atmosphere back to normal.

4th May

Look through the window

I walk across the playground at the end of a long afternoon lesson with the dreaded 10a. They have been very noisy. Before English they have PE. This means half of them are exhausted, the other half exhilarated. It is impossible to interest them in a language lesson. I am saved by the bell. For some reason, when I am walking across the playground on the way to the station, I look back through the classroom window. The next lesson has already started. It is Latin. They are sitting at their tables. The teacher is standing at the front. There seems to be utter peace and quiet.

So they can be quiet. I suspect the more humane you try to be as a teacher the more you suffer. Clearly the answer lies in being less friendly. This morning I heard the PE teacher yell across the corridor. I have done that too. Quite frequently, in fact. Yelling seems to rub off. Or is it better to suffer and survive with the spirit intact?

15th June

Cast in the role of a policeman

I have started to write this diary with the aim of distancing myself from the process of being taken over by the institution and its values. I wanted to make sure that I did not simply become a teacher like all the others. Or, if it could not be helped, I wanted at least to keep a record of what was happening.

So, for the record: once inside school I am cast in the role of a policeman, telling pupils to leave the building during break, challenging adolescents who have disappeared for a smoke, controlling homework, penalizing those who haven't done it and making sure nobody cheats in a test. Once on the job, it all seems necessary and logical. I want to enjoy the same respect as the Latin teacher behind the window. Respect has its price, though. Friends tell me they notice the tension in me. I am on the look-out for potential attacks. I have to defend myself, challenging adolescents even outside the hours I am paid to do so.

20th June

Drama

Today's bit of drama had, of course, never been planned. 10a kept looking for my weak spots. They found them. It was the afternoon lesson. It had taken a long long time to establish any order and I had just about succeeded in getting them to do an exercise, when a boy from the second row of seats got up to open the window. The windows are, admittedly, difficult to open. The boy was pulling it very hard but did not manage to open it. Meanwhile the class's interest had switched to him. They started to laugh. The more he struggled with the window, the more hysterical their laughter became. At that point I lost my nerve. I just could not face another round of calming them down. Something drastic had to be done. I wrote the name of the boy who had gone to the window in the register (which means there will be some disciplinary consequence) and sent him out of the classroom. His neighbour burst into more hysterical laughter. At which point Oliver joined in the action, protesting I was being grossly unjust. While I was at it I wrote down his name as well and sent him out, too. Others came to his aid, telling me I had picked on the wrong person. By this time rationality had gone. I shouted that there was going to be no more discussion.

22nd June

Assessing the damage

Assessing the damage. They show me how disappointed they are in me. Perhaps it was the wrong thing to do. It is pretty exhausting to bear the consequences. On the other hand, on a technical level, it has been quiet for the last two lessons. When I warn them, my warning is taken seriously. However, my shining self-image as a liberal teacher ('I'm able to manage without formal punishment') is dented. I am trying to edge away from being tough. It's not what I am anyway.

Analysis

Introduction

What was the theme of my first year as a language teacher? It was neither the distinction between learning and acquisition, nor that between fluency and accuracy, it was classroom control. What was on my mind was not the methodological subtleties we had been preoccupied with during training, but whether Oliver from 10a would have a good day or not. My efforts, difficulties and failures to achieve classroom control loom large in this first batch of entries. They do so because episodes like *Fell flat on its face* had quickly shown me that planning an ideal lesson with ideal material presented in the ideal sequence of learning steps was one thing, but that realizing such a lesson in a class of thirty and against a constant background of little disturbances was quite another. Only if I was able to control these disturbances would I be able to teach.

Achieving control was, of course, far from easy. The image I have of myself as a teacher during this first year is one of a person trying to survive, who is at the mercy of the situation and its uncontrollable web of influences and pressures. I was up against a situation that – much as I wanted to make it controllable – seemed almost inherently beyond control. Neither the individuals I was facing (Oliver's temper tantrums) nor the group as a whole were predictable. I could take nothing for granted, not even the acknowledgement that I was the teacher (see the episode *A new pupil*). There seemed to be a hidden logic behind the course of events frustrating my intentions, but I could not at the time discover what it was (*Missed the vital clue*).

Not being able to control the uncertainties of the classroom was in every respect stressful. Behind the physical strain was the emotional strain of having to weather conflicts with adolescents (*Little skirmishes at the beginning* and *Drama*) in which I found myself unwillingly behaving in a way I did not approve of (meting out formal punishment in the *Drama* episode). During these initial difficulties colleagues were – with the odd exception – of little help. Staffroom relations for me as a beginner were almost as uncertain as classroom relations (see the episode *Community of moaners*).

This part of the chapter will take another look at the sufferings reported in the first selection of diary entries. It will try to analyse and explain what teachers' work is about. Because of their importance in both the episodes and in methodology books, discipline and classroom control will be the point of departure for this analysis. A more detailed discussion of the situation teachers work in seems necessary because understanding it is fundamental for any changes and innovations to be effective. My argument has the following steps:

1 It starts out from the importance discipline and *classroom control* have for teachers.
2 It then describes the *uncertainties of the teaching situation* as one of the factors responsible for this.
3 As a next step it looks at the *strain* uncertainty causes for teachers.
4 In a first summary it shows how the characteristics of teachers' work can become *obstacles to innovation*.

5 Finally, the students' point of view is considered and *student alienation* as one danger of too rigidly controlled classes is discussed.

1 First discipline, then teaching

Generations of teachers have got their priorities straight: first discipline, then teaching. Practitioners see classroom control as probably their most urgent task, because, in Hargreaves' words, without it the classroom soon becomes a 'circus without a ringmaster ... and the teacher will become rapidly exhausted and demoralised'. (Hargreaves 1972 p234)

In an article published in *The Guardian* a language teacher praises her new school. At the school where she had taught before she had felt 'battered, bruised and disillusioned' by her difficulties in grappling with totally undisciplined and mixed classes. At her new school things were much better. This was due to improved discipline. She claims to have learnt useful new techniques from her colleagues, who have got their priorities straight:

'Don't try and get them to like you. They've got their own friends.'
'We don't care if you don't teach a word of Spanish for most of the lesson provided by the end you've got control.'
'Don't even let them into the classroom until you've got them quiet.'
'Make them stand until they've shifted their cases and gear under the table.'

(*The Guardian* 29 January 1991 p21)

There is, of course, more than anecdotal evidence for the central role of classroom control. Those who have studied 'teachers' work'[1] from the more detached vantage point of sociological research come to much the same conclusion:

... there is universal agreement that the teacher must establish and keep sovereignty over classroom affairs ... beginning teachers soon learn that if their capacity to maintain 'classroom control' is in doubt they may be fired. (Lortie 1975 p51)

Classroom control is not only basic in the sense that it is a task to be solved before teaching can begin. Various studies on the sociology of the teaching profession have shown that it is so central that it shapes and moulds teachers' beliefs, if not their personalities. Connell's (1985) study mentions teachers, 'well on in their careers', who seemed 'tired and blunted' people. He suspects that it has indeed been the custodial aspect of their work, ie year after year of coercing kids to do things they do not want to do, that has helped to make those teachers the way they are. Indeed, many teachers end up wearing a mask in order to establish control (see the episode *Cast in the role of a policeman*). The role behaviour that follows from this may take over to such an extent that it becomes a threat to a teacher's personal identity. Claxton (1989) quotes a teacher writing in *Time Out*:

I decided that I had to get out of teaching when, walking down the corridor, I heard myself screaming 'tie!' at some kid I didn't even know. I suddenly realized that I wasn't myself any more ... (Claxton 1989 p33)

---

1 So the title of a study by Connell (1985) which has given this chapter its name and which will frequently be referred to.

Research about the socialization of teachers has studied the process of how an individual makes the transition from being a student to being a member of the teaching profession. It is the necessity to establish control which such studies consider moulds teachers' attitudes. According to Denscombe (1985) teachers are socialized 'on site'. The influence brought to bear on them by the classroom situation is much more powerful than their training, which might have espoused liberal values that cannot be kept up in the actual teaching situation. It is the familiar story of the young idealistic teacher who 'adapts' to the school situation. There is evidence from studies by Lacey (1977) and Zeichner *et al.* (1987) that shows how this happens (although teachers' individual developments are not necessarily predetermined by the institution). Moreover, the acceptance of newcomers by other members of the staff, incidentally a prerequisite for the acceptance of any new ideas they might bring with them, is said to depend on their reputed ability to control classes (Hargreaves 1972 p240). Why is classroom control so high on teachers' agendas?

2 An uncertain situation

Situations of professional practice are, according to Schön (1990 p6), characterized by uncertainty, uniqueness and value conflicts. This is true of professions like medicine, law and architecture. It is also true of teaching. Schön, in fact, singles out teaching as a prime example for uncertainty and contradictory pressures:

> Practitioners are frequently embroiled in conflicts of values, goals, purposes, and interests. Teachers are faced with pressures for increased efficiency in the context of contracting budgets, demands that they rigorously 'teach the basics', exhortations to encourage activity, build citizenship, help students to examine their values. (Schön 1983 pp16–17)

Leuschner and Schirmer (1993), writing about teacher health, also see a basic contradiction in teachers' self-images between demands made by society to act competently, ie to be in control, and a work situation which is inherently uncertain and therefore difficult to control. In a similar vein, Doyle (1979) characterizes the teaching situation as multidimensional, simultaneous, immediate and unpredictable.

The uncertainty of the teaching situation takes various forms. Its most immediate one for the teacher – and experienced every single day – is the many external factors on which the success of a lesson seems to hinge and which are, at the same time, beyond the teacher's control. Classroom situations are unique, because the individuals in the class and the 'chemistry' between them are unique. Teaching two parallel groups often turns out to be a trap because a lesson that has worked in one class fails in the other. With children, who change quickly, unpredictability not only applies to groups but also to the different stages in their development. The change from one stage to the next can happen fast and has to be responded to on the spot. There are no textbook solutions for this. If the textbook or a colleague in the staffroom says 'If in doubt be firm,' this may, without a proper appraisal of the actual situation (as the episode *Community of moaners* showed), lead to completely wrong action. The behaviour of a class often depends on imponderables like its current mood, on what has happened in the preceding lessons, on the weather, time of day, etc. I often went into 10a armed with several scenarios for a clamp-down and was taken by surprise, because the class was, on that particular day and due to some undetectable factor, peaceful and quiet. There is so much teachers have no control over: timetables, rooms, books, etc. It has been shown that often it is the most trivial constraints imposed by the institution and the situation that exert a powerful influence on what happens in the classroom. Practitioners warn the beginner that things like the timetable may make their lives misery: 'A class may be angelic at 9.30 a.m., can be restive by 2 p.m. and positively murderous by 3.30 p.m.' (see the episode *A new pupil*). The timetable, he goes on, 'is so complicated' that 'no one can afford to consider how the results may affect the individual teacher'. (Francis 1975 pp 73–4)

Given a situation that is inherently uncertain, it is understandable that establishing some form of order and control is of immediate importance to teachers. When establishing control, teachers might often manage to appear as powerful figures and as 'masters' of the situation. However, classroom control is essentially not an expression of teacher autonomy but a reaction to the uncertainty and the constraints of a situation that already exists. Connell writes:

> Without condoning the attitudes or practices of genuinely authoritarian characters, it is important to recognise that the disciplinary responses of teachers in general are intelligible and reasonable responses to situations they have been presented with, over which they have (in the short term) limited control. (Connell 1985 p 105)

The uncertainties of teaching go far beyond the actual teaching situation. They are inherent in difficulties in assessing the quality of teachers' work. When has a lesson been successful? What are its short-term and what are its long-term effects? How are long-term effects to be assessed? Are they actually attributable to teaching?

Another source of uncertainty for teachers is the question of what their relationship with a class is to be like. The task facing a teacher is to resolve the dilemma between making a class work within the rules of the institution and, at the same time, taking care of the emotional climate in the classroom. Teachers are supposed to direct a class towards and through a task and at the same time base their work with a class on a relationship with pupils that is both personal and motivating (Lortie 1975 p 152). Indeed, children often say 'I learn for the teacher, because I like him or her.' One teacher interviewed by Lortie clearly expresses the contradiction between establishing control and having a positive emotional relationship with students:

> I like to be their friend and yet to know when hilarity and fun stops. I think they know where the line goes ... You have controlled discipline all the time. (Lortie 1975 p 154)

Emotions are the substance of children's life. Emotions are therefore the substance of teaching children. The episodes *Tunnel vision*, *Oliver* and *Drama* tell the tale of how quickly kids can turn the classroom into a turmoil of emotions in which it is impossible to stay detached or, indeed, to make any rational decisions. On the surface, it may seem as if situations of this kind are isolated incidents. They are not. They are part of the job. Children show their emotions more openly than adults. Dealing with emotions is therefore more than just an initial barrier to teaching that has to be got out of the way before the actual instruction can begin (Connell 1985). I am still amazed to what extent colleagues come back from classes charged with emotions – almost exclusively negative ones – finding it hard to get rid of them in the short intervals in the staffroom. Emotions are, as Connell claims, in a very literal sense teachers' work:

> Keeping order, and getting the kids to learn, both require operating on the emotions of the kids through the emotions of the teacher. (Connell 1985 p117)

This, incidentally, often causes difficulties for the beginning teacher. One of the authors in a handbook for student teachers in Germany (Reichert 1982 p466) pinpoints the emotional aspect of teaching as the one that often escapes the beginner. It is argued that beginning teachers, when encountering difficulties in the classroom, tend to respond to them with strategies they are familiar with from university or college. Such strategies are in essence cognitive ones, eg more and better preparation (as described in the episode *Forms for the future*). In following these strategies they pay too much attention to the 'task side' of their job and therefore fail to address what might have caused their difficulties in the first place: the emotional relations in the classroom. Their increased effort may well yield no better result because it has the wrong target.

3 Physical and emotional strains

Lortie characterizes teachers' work in the following way:

> Teachers do 'people work', but they do it under somewhat special conditions. Three peculiarities are evident: the low degree of voluntarism in the teacher–student relationship, the problem of extracting work from immature workers, and the grouped context of teacher endeavors. (Lortie 1975 p137)

No wonder this task is perceived as strenuous. In fact there is ample evidence to show how strenuous it is. Connell (1985) ironically comments:

> School teaching is by common repute an easy job, a 'soft cop' with short hours, long holidays, and little physical exertion. Conservative politicians and right-wing professors of philosophy can rely on having an audience whenever they get an uncontrollable urge to do some teacher-bashing. (Connell 1985 p115)

Health statistics, too, show that teaching is by no means a soft option. The exhaustion teachers feel and the pressures on them are real. In a recent summary of research on the subject of teacher health Leuschner and Schirmer quote statistics showing a significantly higher incidence of nervous and heart diseases among teachers than among the average population. Not being able to control the uncertainties of the classroom may lead to various symptoms of physical illness like not being able to sleep or loss of voice. The episode *Flu* is just one of the regular occasions when the annual spell of infections, voice trouble and general exhaustion at the end of term (exam time, handing in of reports) produce a state in which on certain days I simply could not face going into the classroom. As one of the teachers interviewed by Connell said:

Do you like your job?
Yes, I do. I find it a big strain.
What is it about it that's a strain?
I find the psychological and even physical confrontation with the kids constantly. In the first year of teaching, the strain is immense. If you care at all about what you're doing, the strain is immense. (Connell 1985 p116)

Despite the hundreds of personal encounters teachers have in their classrooms they work, as a rule, on their own (see the episode *Closed doors*). The classic constellation in teaching is a teacher 'confronting' a class. Teachers may not see their isolation exclusively in negative terms. Much as they may suffer from being deprived of contacts at their workplace, there is something to be said for privacy, especially if things go wrong. Close the classroom door behind you and be your own boss. Yet it is doubtful how autonomous teachers are at their workplace. Are they really their own boss? Haven't, for instance, people further up the hierarchy the right to enter the privacy of the classroom whenever they wish? Episodes like *But what would a visitor see?* illustrate the fears associated with occasions when teachers are 'visited'. Even for experienced teachers inspections are occasions of unease.

Rather than being splendid, teachers' isolation is therefore at best ambivalent. It might, on the one hand, afford them some degree of autonomy; on the other hand, teachers are, whenever they face problems within that sphere, on their own. The sanctity of the classroom, too, is only an apparent one. What happens there is not much of a secret either, because ultimately the school will know about it through unofficial channels of communication. The stories that go through such channels – especially those about discipline problems – add up to a teacher's 'reputation', which in turn can become an important factor in being able to establish control (as the episode *As a known entity* at the beginning of Chapter 2 will show). Several studies (Hargreaves 1972, Bohnsack 1984) mention unofficial hierarchies in the staffroom that are established according to such reputations. Hargreaves advises beginners to gain their colleagues' respect by solving their discipline problems themselves. In the episode *Look through the window* I felt my place in this hierarchy was far from the top and I consequently envied my colleague, who apparently did not have any problems with classroom control.

Why did I not go to him, ask him if I could sit in on his class and see how he taught? Colleagues would seem to be the most obvious source of information for beginners to learn from. And yet they aren't. One episode in Chapter 2 (*Fun to watch*) will show that I had to travel far afield in order to share an experienced teacher's knowhow. Why was this not possible in my own school? Was it the indifference of those who had the expertise and sat next to me in the staffroom? I believe not. For what can be more flattering than if your expertise is in demand? It was, in fact, here where the problem lay. It was some unwritten rule of the staffroom which precluded the transfer of expertise. I found this rule rather reminiscent of that in force in a school class. 'Don't be a swot. Don't show you are good.' Hargreaves makes the effects of such rules on teachers explicit:

> This [ie teachers'] exhaustion is exacerbated by the high degree of pro-
> fessional isolation among teachers. By this I do not mean that teachers lack
> friends. I refer rather to the non-supportive relationships among teachers,
> which leave each one to solve his own problems. The informal rule among
> teachers is that every teacher is king in his own classroom. Any interference
> that threatens that autonomy is not to be tolerated ... Colleagues who know
> that a teacher is in difficulties are hesitant to offer help, partly because that is
> to suggest incompetence, and partly because it is to violate professional
> autonomy. Teachers bear their stress in painful isolation. (Hargreaves 1978
> pp 540–1)

This ties in with the episode in which one of my colleagues had 'gone public' on
his difficulties (*Breaking the privacy rule*) and had received no response at all.
The study by Bohnsack (1984) also observes that an open discussion of teachers'
personal difficulties with a class is taboo even in a meeting supposed to solve these
difficulties. This tendency not to 'betray' (Hargreaves 1978 p 540) problems to
colleagues leads to a situation where the teacher's isolation is reinforced.

4 Obstacles to change

All these factors, ie the importance of control, the uncertainty of the teaching
situation as well as the various strains of the job, have a tendency to produce an
atmosphere which is not conducive to change and innovation. In my view they
lead to two main obstacles putting themselves in the way of real innovation in the
school classroom.

The first follows directly from what has just been said about the isolation teachers
work in. This isolation leads to a lack of a free and in-depth exchange of opinions
and ideas. For teachers a school day is divided up into long teaching slots during
which formal relations with a group are required, followed by relatively short
breaks during which contacts with colleagues are possible. Because of the sheer
scarcity of time during breaks the opportunities for such contacts are very limited.
Moreover, starting discussions about the job is risky, because staffroom relations
are a precarious matter. For many teachers the staffroom is – despite its peculiar
code of conduct – a sanctuary from the confrontations and pressures of the job.
As one teacher in Germany, quoted in Bohnsack's study, put it:

> I can only survive at school because of the breaks, because it's then that I
> have contact with the others. If I didn't have that, I don't know whether I'd
> still be a teacher. (Wesemann 1984 p 55, my translation)

This statement shows how important informal relationships in the staffroom can
be for the emotional well-being of teachers. Teachers hesitate to put the few 'off-
stage' occasions of their school day at risk, least of all by bringing up controversial
pedagogical issues. Bohnsack's study found that staff studiously avoided pedagogical issues in their contacts. This was especially true for meetings on classes and
students. Possible conflicts of substance were kept at bay by conducting the discussion entirely at the level of formal regulations and grades.

A second obstacle to innovation is teachers' need for stability and control. Those
doing research on language learning and teaching (cf Widdowson 1984) demand

that practitioners should be open to challenge. However justified such demands may be theoretically, it should not be forgotten that teachers work in a situation which is in itself a constant challenge and therefore fosters a craving for some form of stability and security rather than an openness to doubts. Unfortunately, student autonomy will initially often appear as a threat to this stability. A lot of innovative attempts in language teaching – both communicative language teaching and the 'humanistic' approaches to be discussed later in this book – have learner autonomy at their core. However, if approaches that rely on learner autonomy are put to work in a school context they must work in an environment where control features prominently and where the granting of autonomy may therefore be perceived as a threat to classroom control.

The prominence given to classroom control together with the isolation in which teachers' work is carried out also affects perceptions and attitudes between teachers and students. According to Grell (1974 p131) teachers tend to see what they do primarily in terms of their own intentions and not in terms of what these intentions do to pupils. Buber (see Chapter 3) once demanded that educators should 'experience the other side' (Buber 1986 [1953] pp43–4). It seems inherently difficult for teachers to do just this, ie leave their role and watch what is going on in their classroom. It is in the face of such difficulties that seeing what happens in the classroom from a different perspective is essential. Such a change of perspective is attempted in the next section (and, on a larger scale, in Chapter 3).

5 Student alienation

Discipline and control have so far only been seen from the point of view of teachers, ie in terms of their priorities and intentions. But how about what actually happens in the classroom? What are the consequences of these priorities for students? In this section I want to complement the teacher's view of the classroom with a look at research on classroom interaction. Having looked, so far, at issues affecting school in general, ie almost every subject, classroom control will now be discussed with particular reference to language teaching.

Ever since Sinclair and Coulthard's *Towards an Analysis of Discourse* (1975), classroom discourse has been a favourite object of study for discourse analysts because it is well structured and ideally (!) one person controls who talks and when. For this very reason it was feasible for Sinclair and Coulthard to take a piece of teacher-centred discourse and derive from it a well-ordered hierarchy of acts:

> With these and many other problems inherent in conversation we decided it would be more productive to begin with a more simple type of spoken discourse, one which has a much more overt structure, where one participant has acknowledged responsibility for the direction of the discourse, for deciding who shall speak when, and for introducing and ending topics.
> (Sinclair and Coulthard 1975 p6)

Looking at Sinclair and Coulthard's analysis leaves us in no doubt as to how teacher-centred school lessons are. Many studies that have been carried out subsequently show that classroom interaction is almost exclusively led by the teacher. Control, therefore, is not only something that is part of teachers' values and wishes, it is a prominent feature of observed classroom interaction. Language teaching is, of course, no exception. Language lessons appear to be one of the places where teachers exercise a particularly high degree of control. Subjects like literature or social studies may make it easier for teachers and students to approach a text or a topic on a more equal footing. With questions of grammar, correctness or lexical meaning it is a different matter. Here it is quite clearly the teacher who is the expert. Consider the kind of 'discourse' this may lead to. The following is a piece of data taken from a language lesson and quoted by Ehlich (1986):

> Teacher: Now. What is the English name for physical education?
> Pupil 1: PE.
> Pupil 2: PE.
> Pupil 3: PE.
> T: No! The English name, not the abbreviation, not the short word.
> Pupils: whispering.
> Teacher: Who remembers?
> Pupils: coughing.
> Teacher: Some of our classes have it in the afternoon?
> Silence.
> Teacher: It is sports!
> Pupils: Sports!
> Teacher: Yes, it is sports.
> (Ehlich 1986 p 27)

For a long time now language-teaching theory has been all for communicating and discourse. Coursebooks abound in 'over to you' bubbles. And yet a considerable number of language lessons observed in schools still resemble the above exchange. The communication in it goes through one central switchboard, the teacher. As a piece of communication it must sound almost absurd to an outsider. Someone is asking a question to which he/she already knows the answer. The rules of normal communication seem subverted. It may be argued that these are 'teachers' questions' asked with the purpose of easing the students, in a Socratic fashion, towards a solution. I doubt whether the above exchange could be called Socratic. It looks more like a ritual guessing game in which the teacher acts as a less than impartial arbiter. What is right is decided by the teacher. The decision – sports or PE – seems arbitrary to the observer. What the students answer is not wrong. It just does not fit the teacher's expectations.

It is the structure of the subject that makes language lessons even more prone to such exchanges than others. A foreign language has to be presented in a much stricter sequence than other subjects (cf Sauer 1985). One step implies a number (often a great number) of preceding steps. It is like a ladder. You need step A before you can go on to step B. Subjects with a structure of this kind have a greater affinity with tight control than others and indeed Bohnsack's study particularly mentions languages together with maths as one of the more rigorous subjects at school. Given all this, plus the fact that language teaching in schools is still to a vast extent about correctness of form and vocabulary, it is clear that teacher control, insistence on correction, etc will feature prominently in language classes. The rigour of the subject has, incidentally, long been known and lamented. Herbert Spencer, in philosophizing which knowledge is worth acquiring, wrote in 1859:

The learning of languages tends, if anything, further to increase the already undue respect for authority. Such and such are the meanings of these words, says the teacher or the dictionary. So and so is the rule in this case, says the grammar. By the pupil these dicta are received as unquestionable. His constant attitude of mind is that of submission to dogmatic teaching. And a necessary result is a tendency to accept without inquiry whatever is established. (Spencer 1966 [1859] p40)

Wagner (1983) has shown with a corpus of actual lessons that Spencer would not be too far off the mark for today's language classes in schools. According to Wagner's observations, a lot of language teaching consists of teacher-centred guessing games. He has looked at both elementary and advanced language classes in Danish schools and comes up with a rather scathing account of communication in the language classroom, characterizing its various stages as 'guess the right ending' (beginners), 'guess the right word' (intermediate), 'guess what interpretation I have in mind' (advanced).

Analysing a segment of a class discussion, in which students and the teacher try to pick up different strands suggested by the topic of a text, he shows how students try to express their own experience, whereas the teacher tries to lead them back to the text. A conflict of interest emerges that leaves the students frustrated (Wagner 1983 pp155–8). Many of my students who wrote evaluations of their language lessons (see Chapter 4) would support Wagner's findings. They are often under the impression that there is no point in them saying anything in certain lessons, because the teacher has decided beforehand what is right and what is wrong. Especially if they make a grammar mistake in what they say, their statement is immediately invalidated by the teacher. (I find this hardly surprising when I look back at my own training and assessment as a teacher, which put great emphasis on correction of student mistakes.) All this has important consequences for student motivation.

If classroom interaction is dominated by the teacher it runs a risk of not involving students any more and therefore of being irrelevant to them. Wesemann's (1984) study claims to have established a link between such problems and the kind of inter-action prevailing in school classrooms. The consequences of this reach further afield than individual lessons. Schools have been accused of failing children because what takes place in the classroom and what is taught there is irrelevant to pupils' needs, so irrelevant indeed that it may well be at the base of 'negative class participation' (a term used by Wadden and McGovern 1991). Studying the reasons behind school fatigue, Wesemann (1984) sees teacher domination of classroom interaction as one barrier to student activation. He argues that the accumulated effect of interaction dominated by assessment and teacher influence is a hidden message to pupils that only those actions and utterances that make sense in terms of the teacher's lesson plan are admissible in the classroom. The hidden curriculum is: only if something is initiated and asked for by the teacher is it part of the lesson. The hidden curriculum may well counteract the purpose of school lessons: learning. Here is an example:

Because a school morning is essentially fragmented and experienced as an alter-nation of lesson time and break time, one crucial and difficult aspect of teachers' work is to make sure that the switch from break time to lesson time takes place.

Not only the episode *Little skirmishes at the beginning* but also numerous classroom observations in Wesemann's study show that it is exactly at the point when the teacher has to make the lesson begin that the situation is prone to conflict. Wesemann reports several episodes of teachers starting their lessons with gestures of threat as a result of which confrontation arose within seconds. Since (as we shall see in Chapter 2) it is during 'first encounters' that the roles in the classroom and the 'key' of the interaction are defined, such first encounters influence what happens in the remainder of the lesson (see also the episode *Community of moaners*, where the wrong key for the interaction was set mistakenly). If the beginning of a lesson is characterized by little skirmishes, gestures of threat or an element of assessment – and this was the case for many of the lessons observed in Wesemann – this has an influence on the aims pursued in this lesson. In the lessons observed in Wesemann's study the purpose of marking homework, ie giving feedback, had – in the face of discipline problems – often been 'abused' as an opportunity to assess and grade pupils. Once established, such mechanisms led to pupil attitudes and expectations that frustrated attempts to help them learn. A teacher's attempts to help students on an individualized basis during the lesson entailed, for instance, a strong risk of losing control over the rest of the class, because the class had been trained not to pay attention unless under close supervision.

Later in this book I will report about my attempts to have a phase at the beginning of a lesson during which I have a short conversation with individual students (see Chapter 7). Such a beginning seems sensible both in terms of language practice and students' needs. Time and again I heard and read in students' evaluations how positive they had found a phase in which they got individual attention and had, if only for a few moments, the opportunity not to speak about the text but about themselves. Such a beginning to a lesson is, however, not easy to put into practice, because it takes place against a background of 32 individuals who become restive as soon as the teacher focuses on one of them. My individual conversations at the beginning were therefore regularly punctuated by disciplinary moves directed towards the rest of the class.

Ehlich (1986) quotes the transcript of a lesson in which the teacher collects pupils' contributions to a question on the blackboard. The teacher takes up one contribution and tries to elaborate on it. Surprisingly the student who made the contribution turns to her neighbour, starts talking to her, and shows no interest whatever in what is happening to her own contribution.

The teacher comments:

> It happens very often that a pupil gives you part of the solution to a problem, but is not interested in the rest. They ask you a question, you try to answer it and as you open your mouth they turn to their neighbour. (Ehlich 1986 p 25, my translation)

For this student (and many others) participating in the lesson has been reduced to following the rules of a game in which all you have to do is show you are taking part in the official part of classroom transactions (see also Eric in the episode *As long as it isn't grammar*). This means that teacher control – or at least too much of it – can alienate students from what is happening in the classroom. They no longer see it as their own enterprise. Given the pressures exercised by the institution, their lack of voluntarism may take subtle forms. It may be an attitude of 'consumerism' that expects the teacher to hand whatever is to be learnt to them on a plate. It is, in many cases, a view of lessons in which learning is only of minor importance.

6 Conclusion

In this first chapter I have looked at various aspects of classroom control. It has been a chapter on predominantly negative experiences. It had to be. There is no point in painting pictures of school practice in which students and teachers are busy accentuating the positive and pinning humanistic posters on the wall. Reality, at least mine, was different. If innovation in the classroom is to be effect-ive and if new ideas are to reach the grassroots level, this reality, especially its more burdensome aspects, has to be taken into consideration. Teachers' reality is governed by institutional constraints and educational considerations. The importance of the educational context in which language teaching takes place was, incidentally, seen quite early by proponents of the communicative approach:

> ... a command of spontaneous speech can only be acquired in relatively favourable educational environments. Spontaneous speech is the product of interaction between individuals. Teacher–pupil interaction cannot be enough. In any normal-sized class, since only one pupil–teacher exchange can take place at a time, neither the quantity nor the intensity is to any degree adequate to develop the desired skill. This can only be done through pupil–pupil interaction so that numerous exchanges can take place simul-taneously and the continuing active engagement of every learner is ensured. This demands a situation in which the teacher is free and willing to break down the conventional organisation of the class ... Overall this suggests an educational environment in which innovation and flexibility are encouraged ... It is also worth noting that the educational philosophy that permits this degree of freedom to the individual teacher and encourages the learners to participate fully in the direction of their language learning is not compatible with attitudes towards education that are found in some parts of the world. (Wilkins 1983 pp36–7)

Given this acknowledgement of how important the educational context is for the success or failure of a language-teaching approach, it seems astonishing that it has received such scant attention in the literature on methodology. Indeed, I often get the impression that methodology is presented as if only ideally behaved classes existed (consider the episodes *Fell flat on its face* and *Unbearable perfection* as examples of the gulf between what is considered an ideal lesson and what is possible in day-to-day teaching). The editor of the *English Language Teaching Journal*, reporting on an international conference, wrote:

> At the final round table, the panel of well-known experts, all with extensive lists of publications in our field, was asked by a teacher how they would handle a particular 'discipline' problem. The questioner described her problem carefully and sensitively. The panel was all but stunned into silence. (Whitney 1991 p 95)

In short, classroom management and questions of discipline seem to belong to a completely different department from methodology. Yet the diaries give ample evidence of how ideal methodology did not stand the test of everyday conditions at school, because the lessons it generated assumed classes and conditions that did not exist.

Chapter 2 **Coping with discipline**

Diary

10th September

As a known entity

Second year. I take over a new group. This time it is 6c. They seem to know me well by word of mouth. They were briefed by the parallel group I taught last year. I enter the classroom as a known entity. What I do, especially the routines[2] I follow, are not new to them (as they were for last year's classes). Rather they are proof of theories about me established long before I first entered the room. I tell them there will be a weekly word test. They knew there would be. No arguing. At the same time, I find out how many little routines, how much tacit understanding about turn allocation and discipline had developed between my old class and myself last year. This web of mutual understanding and co-operation will have to be rebuilt. It will take time. The initial fight for quietness and control has to be gone through all over again but this time it seems less threatening. I know what it is like. I know I have mastered it before and I know it will not last forever. The first lesson is indeed a long struggle for silence. Some of them almost seemed grateful when I said I was going to ask the class to stand up at the beginning for the first few weeks.

13th September

A few irregular verbs

I ask them a few irregular verbs. They hardly know any of them. Had they finished the book? Yes, but they remembered very little of it.

14th September

If in doubt, act quickly

Yesterday I tested them on irregular verbs; today they tested me. Not on grammar but on my house rules. A boy in the first row of seats took out a comic and leisurely started reading it. Sitting in the front he was, or thought he was, in a dead angle of my field of vision. Luckily I noticed and could react. I looked at him. He looked at me. Without interrupting what I was saying, I made a gesture 'put it away'. He seemed to have been waiting for such a reaction.

I had this rule about discipline: when a pupil is about to disrupt the class, I observe him/her until I am absolutely certain my suspicion is well founded. Students like Oliver, who always claimed they had been treated unjustly, had trained me to do so. The only problem was that by the time I was positively sure I was justified in intervening another ten students would have drifted off and control would be

---

2 I will explain some of them in Chapter 7.

irretrievable. It then took an enormous effort to direct the class back to the task again. I have changed my approach to 'if in doubt, act quickly'.

13th October

A harmless question

Grade 5. I started the lesson with a harmless question: who can retell the story you had to read for today? Mark volunteered. But the story he told us was something completely different from what I thought it should be. Funnily enough, there were no protests from the class. Gradually it dawned on me that I must have got the page wrong and prepared the wrong passage. While he was speaking, I replanned the lesson. It ended up going surprisingly well. I set them (really had to set them) the task: 'Retell the story in such a way that even someone who has not read the story would understand it.' As I was the one who had not read the text, I had to ask lots of 'real' questions and listen carefully to their answers.

14th October

We suddenly had enough time

I try to be more realistic in my planning and in my expectations. Today I had started doing a simple transformation exercise with them. Ten minutes would have seemed enough for it. It turned out they did not understand what they were supposed to do. We got stuck. The rest of my plan seemed seriously under threat. For a few moments I watched my lesson going to pieces. I could see the class getting restive. And so it would have, if I had not forced myself to do something about it. As yesterday's lesson had shown me that improvisation might save the day, I did one more item in order not to appear to be breaking off in panic and then made a measured retreat. I told the class we would do the remaining items in tomorrow's lesson. I went on to the next item on my plan. True enough, this was retreat. But it stopped the atmosphere of despair that was starting to creep in. We suddenly had enough time. I could get through the rest of my plan in a more relaxed way. This was probably more important than finishing the exercise.

11th November

I can breathe

With 10a (now 11a) I have gone over to spending the afternoon lessons in the lab. I have prepared worksheets with listening comprehension tasks. They work through the tapes individually. Preparing the worksheets takes a lot of time and the exercises are not very popular. But the class actually works. And so, much to my surprise, does Oliver. However difficult he may be to talk to in a situation when I stand in front of the class in the role of the teacher (whom he sees as the incarnation of adult power which is to be defied), he is now quite happy to direct the energy he usually puts into disrupting my lessons towards a task. With the imposition of authority removed he sits over his piece of paper and works hard. Many of the others do so, too. As far as discipline goes the lab lessons are a truce. Confrontation has been reduced. I can breathe.

9th December

I want to work with my friends

Today I tell grade 6 to work in groups of four. They are to read a piece of dialogue in groups and then act it out in front of the class. Hardly have I said they are to work in groups (each group corresponding to one row of seats) than pandemonium breaks out. In one row of seats there are only three. I put a fourth student into the group. The boy bluntly refuses. 'I want to work with my friends.' His four friends have formed another group. There is no place for a fifth one. The noise level is rising. It is like a chain reaction. I have to leave the question of which group the boy can join. I am shouting at the top of my voice, half waiting for one of the other teachers to come in and complain. No one does. I leave the lesson thinking that I've had enough of learner autonomy and liberal methods.

20th December

What a fool

I am still used to measuring my success as a teacher in terms of the silence I am able to produce. I still remember my RE teacher in secondary school. After I had left school we once met and he told me one of his early maxims as a teacher, which was 'My classes must be so quiet that you can hear a pin drop.' 'What a fool I was,' he added twenty years later.

8th January

One more try

New year resolutions. It has occurred to me that, so far, I have always reacted to difficulty with a change of tack. If it goes wrong, try something else. I am beginning to doubt the wisdom of this. What I need is more constancy. Changing from a 'normal' teacher-centred lesson to groupwork obviously involves an element of uncertainty and insecurity both for me and the class. Abandoning such an attempt midway can add to uncertainty. Therefore: fewer U-turns. If something goes wrong give it at least one more try. What I also need is something like a ritual that takes place in every single lesson and that is predictable.

15th January

They came back

A few days ago I played a song in grade 6. One I rather liked. The lyrics were quite difficult and the vocabulary was well beyond the grasp of beginners. When they first listened to it they laughed. They said it was impossible for them to sing, because it sounded so strange. I felt a bit disheartened and considered abandoning the whole project. Then I told them to try anyway. We had one halting run-through. I thought I would leave it at that. Today they came back asking me why we didn't go on with that funny song.

16th January

I feel less exposed

With yesterday's encouragement behind me I also gave groupwork a second try. This time I was more careful. I told them what I thought had gone wrong the lesson before and then gave them very strict instructions about noise. I told them it could not be helped if they were in a different group from their friends. I also told them to listen to my instructions until I clapped my hands. Only then were they allowed to begin. Groupwork went much better this time, because they seemed to be a little more used to it. The class did get noisy again. I knew it would, but I was less frightened of it now. I tried to calm them down to a reasonable decibel level, but I also reminded myself that I had decided on this form of work and that I could not expect the same behaviour as in a normal teacher-centred lesson. Bearing this in mind helped me not to get disheartened and to fight the feeling that I had abandoned teaching in this lesson. It was my own will that was behind the lesson. It is becoming clear to me that noisy phases do not mean that from now on all my lessons will end in chaos. There is always a next lesson, good or bad, which can take a different course or at least it is up to me to set a different frame on another occasion. I feel less exposed.

3rd March

Balance sheet

I work with something like a personal balance sheet now. On the one hand I have stopped trying to teach afternoon lessons as if they took place in the morning. This means I expect less in terms of the material I want to cover. On the other hand I spare myself many conflicts that can't be won. Is this retreat? Probably not, as long as the morning lessons go all right.

20th June

I split up a sentence

7a got noisy today. I split up a sentence into the words it contains, 33 in all. They all have to learn the sentence by heart. Then each pupil in the class gets one word. They have to find their place in a long row of pupils representing the original sequence of words in the sentence. Then the words are spoken so that the original sentence is 'reassembled'.

What worked well: I check on the first ones who say they know the sentence by heart. They then check on the other ones. It is debatable how much grammar, pronunciation, words, etc they learn in such an exercise, but the exercise changes the mood of the class. Otherwise it might have quickly turned into boredom, inattention, possibly confrontation. Escaping this was the overriding priority.

14th July

Ghostwriters

Talking about confrontation. Today I collected essays I had set in grade 12 a fortnight ago. I started marking them in the afternoon. A lot of good work. More good work. What Holger and Jens have written is even better. It is, in fact, of native quality. This is something they have not achieved in any written task before. It is the last piece of work they are to hand in before the final assessment. They are both on the border of failing the year. I suspect they had their essays written by someone else. So much for freedom and creativity. If I give them top marks, this distorts their overall grade. Their other marks are all much lower. With hindsight I should have known what kind of temptation I have created. Both the nature and the timing of the task make it prone to 'ghostwriting'. Students are worried about their grade at the end of the year and for some of them the essay grade is their last hope. Allowing outside help is probably the price to be paid for this less controlled form of work. On the other hand, if it is to be allowed, it should be done openly, for after all, there were those who only used their own resources. Justice is a horrible goddess to worship, I know, but for the sake of my authority, I have to do something about it. If the class finds out that I am giving top marks for work that has so obviously been written by a friendly native, this is no good. There are numerous Sherlock Holmes scenarios going through my mind, most of them ending with a trial. Which is exactly what I don't want to happen, because, by and large, the essays have gone well and seem a sensible type of task.

15th July

Justice

It took me a long time to come up with a solution. I tried it this morning. Instead of simply handing back the corrected essays, I asked the class to take ten minutes and write down from memory what they remembered of their essay. After initial protests all of them started writing. I collected the papers. Afterwards Holger and Jens came to me. Each of them had handed in a paper with a German text. They said they had created the contents of their essays themselves but had asked a native speaker to help them. I had not, they said, expressly forbidden this. I agreed. This raised the question of grades. I put the matter to the class. A heated debate followed. Holger and Jens claimed others had used outside help too, like dictionaries, books, etc. The 'others' protested and said they might have used help but had put a lot of time and effort into the essay because they saw it as a chance to improve their grade.

I told the class that awarding fair grades was an impossible task for me to solve under such circumstances. They accepted this. I said I had noted down an impressionistic grade for every essay but that I was lacking any real information as to how much help individual students had got. Only they had this knowledge. I therefore handed them back their essays with my corrections and comments and asked them to decide on their own grades. They did so in tense silence. The grades they suggested seemed in most cases realistic, in some cases rather on the low side. So I didn't play Sherlock Holmes after all.

22nd July

Fun to watch

Holiday. I went north to visit Peter, who has been a teacher for about twenty years. His school breaks up later. Because I was a friend from far away rather than a colleague at the same school, he took me with him into his classroom.

He was great fun to watch. There is nothing more stimulating than seeing someone who teaches well. What I learn is not so much method but behaviour. What I see are reactions, like when he wakes up a pupil who is about to doze off by putting his hand on his shoulder – quite lightly and matter-of-fact. What I see are gestures: how he invites someone to speak. It is such little things (Buber: 'the slightest lifting of a finger') that make all the difference. It is an annoying thought that good lessons are, in a way, 'wasted' on those who do not need them, ie inspectors, supervisors, etc and, for reasons of time and unwritten rules of the profession, not accessible to those who do need them.

Analysis

Introduction

The message coming from the above batch of entries is, at long last, a less gloomy one. Something can be done. We need not be as deterministic as some of the research findings in the last chapter might have suggested.

There is the familiar story of the liberal young teacher who gets frustrated by reality and then makes a U-turn on all his/her liberal ideals. This happens. On the other hand, although there is 'internalized adjustment', ie the teacher takes over the values of the environment he/she works in, and although there is 'strategic compliance', ie a teacher ends up in 'inner emigration', there are teachers who are capable of 'strategic redefinition' (cf Lacey 1977), ie teachers who are able to salvage at least some of their ideals, incorporate them into their everyday work at school and change this work.[3] The constraints of the teaching situation at school may, at first, be overwhelming; at the same time a teacher's development is not preordained by them. Studies on classroom interaction by Ehlich (1986), Bohnsack (1984) or Wagner (1983), who are otherwise merciless in their criticism of school teaching, take great care to argue against any form of determinism.

However, even those who manage to change the situation at school must do so on the terms laid down by the institution. In other words: they must survive. This is what this chapter is about. Having criticized the mechanisms of school interaction so rigorously at the end of the previous chapter, it may seem natural to make suggestions as to how these might be changed. I will postpone such suggestions for one chapter for the simple reason that the most urgent task for the beginner is coming to terms with the teaching situation as he/she finds it (as Connell 1985 p 105 wrote: 'situations they have been presented with').

Numerous competent guides to survival in the classroom exist. Some of them (a rather personal selection) will be looked at here with the aim of relating their advice to the episodes in the first part of this chapter and, as a next step, placing it into a wider context than the immediate necessities of survival. Survival is not and cannot be an end in itself. All the same it is essential.

The episodes in this chapter describe a number of changes and discoveries in my second year:

The first was that time helped. Increased practice, more routine and experience helped me to get some of my initial difficulties out of the way. In particular, having got through the first year made a difference (see the episode *As a known entity*). By the beginning of my second year I had learnt certain tricks of the trade, as the episode *If in doubt, act quickly* shows.

Secondly, my self-confidence had increased. I now had a slightly clearer notion of what I wanted and of what I could do. This helped me to be more insistent when introducing something new and to achieve more constancy in my work (see the episodes *One more try, They came back, Balance sheet*).

---

3 It should be added that a study by Zeichner *et al.* (1987) shows that the right environment is of decisive influence for 'strategic redefinition'.

Thirdly, I had become more flexible in what I did in the classroom. This was, among other things, a result of better perceptions of what was going on around me. It increasingly enabled me to find my own solutions to situations that would have got on top of me in my first year (see in particular the episode *Ghostwriters*).

The 'suggestions for survival' that follow are based on these insights. They are centred around four important aspects of classroom control:

1 first encounters between a teacher and a class
2 constancy
3 breathing spaces
4 flexibility

1 First encounters

Missed the vital clue. The episode of the same name in Chapter 1 describing my first meeting with 10a showed that the parameters of the interaction to take place between the class and myself (What would I tolerate? When would I intervene?) were established in a matter of hours. It seemed, retrospectively, as if decisions made – or rather not made – at the very beginning had long-term effects that were difficult to change later. Having said that, the cues on which to act are easily missed, because they are often rather inconspicuous.

Robertson gives an example of the traps someone coming new into a class might fall into:

> The teacher, on entering the room, looks at the pupils and returns a smile from a boy in the front. The boy continues to smile and asks a question:
> 1st pupil: Are you our new teacher, Miss?
> Teacher: (Continuing to smile) That's right. (Another pupil calls out).
> 2nd pupil: Are you strict like Mr Brown was, Miss? (Teacher looks towards him, takes a breath to answer, but another boy calls out to the previous pupil).
> 3rd pupil: He was a nutcase! (Laughter from class).
> Teacher: (No longer smiling, looking at new speaker) Now ... that will do. I'd like your attention please.
> (Robertson 1989 [1981] p32).

Robertson argues that this tiny sequence, lasting less than a minute, might set the key for the lesson to follow. The teacher, by smiling, has put the pupils at ease too early. If the interaction were to continue as it began he/she would soon find it difficult to maintain control over the teaching situation. Robertson reminds his readers of a book with reports by probationary teachers entitled *Don't smile 'till Christmas* (Ryan 1970). The title is said to have served as a motto for many a novice in the classroom.

Research studies mention a honeymoon of one or two lessons during which the students are 'weighing up' the teacher. This is soon followed by a period during which the class more actively explores the 'parameters of control the teacher is seeking to establish' (Robertson 1989 [1981] p51 quoting from Ball 1980) and whether he/she is actually able 'to defend' these parameters. The episode *If in doubt, act quickly* was one such test. It was then that the relationship between me and class was being defined and it was then that I had to act if I wanted to establish my authority. Research literature advises beginners to act quickly and define the situation in their own terms in order to establish their authority as soon as possible, because:

> In establishing the order he has decided upon, the teacher must be fully aware that what happens in the first few encounters with the pupils is likely to establish the relationships which he will have to live with for the rest of his contact with that particular class. (Wadd 1973 quoted in Robertson 1989 [1981] p51)

It should be added that setting the key for the interaction between teacher and class is not only a matter of initial encounters. Almost every phase of a lesson presents the teacher with the task of establishing whether this 'key' is to be one of relaxation or one of serious business (see the remarks on humour at the end of this chapter). It should also be noted that redefining the situation at a later stage is difficult but not impossible.

Defining the situation in the teacher's terms often means quick action. One essential tool for being able to act quickly is knowing the names of the pupils as early as possible. Francis (1975) and many others make a point of getting, in the first lesson, a plan of the seating arrangement in the classroom with all the names. I usually learn the plan by heart and gradually match names to persons. This has turned out to be one of the most basic and important first steps when taking over a class.

Another prerequisite for prompt action is noticing potential difficulties early. Being able to notice what is happening at the various corners of the classroom has been considered an important skill for maintaining classroom control. Kounin (1970) uses the term 'with-it-ness' for this. 'With-it-ness' means the 'proverbial eyes in the back of the teacher's head', ie the ability not to be entirely absorbed with teaching but to monitor alongside how students react. Kounin's term goes back to an empirical study. Hargreaves (1972) adds an element of trickery to it. He gives the following example: a teacher may observe pupils without them noticing it and then comment on their behaviour while looking in the opposite direction. He is thus giving the impression that he/she really does see everything. (I have the lasting memory of a French teacher who never left his desk in the front of the classroom and at the same time, during dictations, told those sitting in the last row when they got their accents wrong.)

Prompt action may seem to a beginning teacher far too pre-emptive. It may well feel like coming down harder than is justified by the class's apparent behaviour. It may, indeed, seem like a bulldozing approach. Yet the 'smiling' incident just quoted shows that it may be little things – a word, a gesture, an oversight – that might turn out to be the real time bombs.

It is often non-verbal signals, like for instance a smile, that are perceived and interpreted by students when exploring the limits of teacher authority. Robertson (1989 [1981]) gives numerous examples of how authority is expressed and perceived through such non-verbal means. A teacher can, for instance, express confidence in his/her authority by 'using pupil territory', ie by not standing glued to the blackboard but by moving around freely between the rows of seats. A more dramatic form of using pupil territory can be to move very close to a student in order to get his/her attention. Non-verbal behaviour should, however, not be threatening or intimidating. Indeed, the gentler it is, the greater its effect. Robertson claims that a teacher's authority expresses itself in a relaxed body posture, facial expression and voice. One example of a 'relaxed' intervention is when a teacher is able to convey feedback on unwanted behaviour to a student without interrupting the lesson. I sometimes managed to get back a group of students' attention by moving to their corner of the room and going on teaching as if nothing had happened. In this way, the class was not disrupted and, at the same time, the change in physical distance got the message across that I did not want them to speak.

Valid as the observations made by Robertson and Hargreaves may be, a word of caution should be added. Given the necessity and urgency of classroom control, suggestions like the above sound reasonable. True enough, it is easier to relax on a rule once it has been established than to re-establish one that has ceased to be binding. This is, in fact, what some of the teachers interviewed by Connell (1985) say: 'Come down hard at first and relax later.' However, it should not be overlooked that Robertson's statements are descriptions of teachers who are already in control. It is subject to discussion whether they are equally valid as instructions, ie whether someone who is genuinely insecure may be able to 'act' as if in authority. This, however, is what the authors advise beginners to do: put on some kind of professional mask. Hargreaves (1972) advocates a certain degree of acting as a temporary measure.

> The contrived performance is a means to an end, namely the establishment of [the teacher's] dominance. It is essentially a *temporary* [his italics] measure ... he will soon be able to drop this mask. (Hargreaves 1972 p238)

Robertson puts it more cautiously. Although in the long run teachers will have to 'earn their authority' by good teaching, it is 'helpful from the outset to behave as if they already have it.' (Robertson 1989 [1981] p58)

I suspect that children's abilities to notice the genuineness of the act are not to be underestimated. In the event, a failed act might do more damage to a beginner's authority than good. Descriptions of non-verbal behaviour should therefore be treated with caution lest they turn into paradoxical imperatives: 'Be relaxed, even when you aren't.'

The previous chapter mentioned some of the sufferings experienced by the beginner when having to act the role of teacher. There is probably a difference between involuntary behaviour which is a result of the pressures of the job and a deliberate attempt to influence a class that might, especially if it is a younger class, be responsive to such acting. One consideration for whether to act or not should certainly be the extent to which the teacher is at ease with doing so. Finally, authority, as opposed to dominance, may express itself in completely different ways from those described so far. Berliner (1987), who studied the differences in 'craft knowledge' that exist between novice teachers and expert teachers, presents an example of how a high degree of self-assuredness enabled one of the teachers interviewed to make his first encounter with the class very personal and to make himself quite 'vulnerable' in such a situation:

I think my prime concern is to allow the students to look at me. In other words, I would want to make myself somewhat vulnerable that [first] day to the kids. So they would know ... what is acceptable behavior and what is not acceptable behavior from my value system ... I think because teaching involves so many humanist attributes that each teacher has to do their own thing and be accepted on their own terms. (Berliner 1987 p74)

Experienced teachers are apparently much less worried about discipline than beginners. 'There was no doubt in their mind, given years of successful experience, that they could manage a class' (Berliner 1987 p74). The course of action described by this teacher may therefore not be open to the beginner. It is, however, worth keeping in mind because the relationship with a class should not only be looked at in terms of establishing teacher control.

2 Constancy

First encounters may be important, but they do not decide everything. Firmness at the beginning is advisable, but there are more ways of expressing firmness and determination than non-verbal language. Both Hargreaves (1972) and Robertson (1989 [1981]) point out that ultimately it is the quality of teaching that will make the difference. Reacting to disciplinary problems as they arise is an urgent matter and therefore has top priority. However, this urgency should not obscure the question of why such problems arose in the first place and how they could be avoided altogether. The following section presents a number of long-term strategies that look beyond any immediate crisis. What are they?

It took me a long time to realize that one pattern of action I was following in the classroom was to change tack whenever anything went wrong. This often resulted in my going from one extreme to another, ie from liberalism to a sudden clampdown. However, the episodes *They came back* and *One more try* show that I gradually learnt that there was something to be said for constancy: I stuck to a course once I had taken it. Doing so sometimes meant doing unpopular things like keeping up the lab exercises. Despite the fact that they did not say so in public, most groups actually wanted consistency. It therefore often paid to stick to my course, because a second try often proved successful (*They came back*). Hargreaves (1972 p249) advises the same for measures related to discipline: give them time to work. For students constancy means the teacher is predictable and this therefore gives them security. (See the episode *As a known entity*, in which the knowledge about what I was likely to do made the beginning with a new class that much easier.)

There are many aspects to being predictable. As far as discipline is concerned, carrying out a threat once it has been made, and provided it has been thought through in advance, may well be a central one. In terms of method it can mean advance orientation (see Chapter 3, p55), clarity, and a set of fixed ingredients possibly presented in a fixed sequence in each lesson (see Chapter 7). All this adds up to the 'web of co-operation' mentioned in the episode *As a known entity*. Wesemann (1984) gives an example of a teacher for whom the fragility of the moment when she had to effect the switch from break time to lesson time at the beginning of a lesson had been removed because she had found the right mixture of predictability and openness:

When there has been a lot of action during break time, and they want to tell me about it, then I say: 'Get a move on, I want to start the lesson, we've got a lot to get through today,' or 'We've got a lot of work to do at the beginning, we'll have more time towards the end, then you can talk.' When I see there has been trouble in the previous lessons ... I raise it as a topic and say 'What happened this morning? Tell me.' Then they start telling me about it and I say 'Five minutes, after that we start the lesson.' (Wesemann 1984 p 73, my translation)

The teacher makes the lesson predictable ('later we'll have more time') and imposes a time limit of five minutes. Both teacher and students can rely on the lesson beginning then. When opening classroom interaction to student concerns, especially with younger classes, it is particularly important to set such limits because otherwise pupils will quickly develop strategies for drawing out such discussions and never letting a lesson begin. This may lead to a situation where discussions about class matters become red herrings and consequently get the unfortunate image of something that can be used to find a way round starting the actual 'business' of the lesson.

3 Breathing spaces

The teacher just quoted describes how she creates little islands of peace for herself at the beginning of her lessons:

When I've entered the room, closed the door, put my briefcase on the desk and when one of the kids is sitting around or standing around in an unacceptable way, then – I usually know them – I raise my eyebrows, trying to say 'This can't be true, that you dare to do that' and he is down from his desk in a flash. Then they start moving towards their seats voluntarily, I usually prepare the OHP, take out my notes and have a quick glance at where I wanted to start. (Bohnsack 1984 p73)

Teaching large classes is, as we have seen, physically strenuous. Exhaustion can make the task of classroom control even more burdensome (see the episode *Short-termism* in Chapter 1). I experienced quite a few discipline breakdowns because I physically no longer had the strength to put up any resistance to pupil interruption. A realistic appraisal of the teaching situation must therefore include the teacher's own state of mind and body. Being aware of this can help one to be realistic as to which action one has the strength to take at a given moment. If exhaustion threatens to set in preventive action should be taken and periods of rest and breathing spaces should be created if at all possible. Such phases can, for instance, be created in the middle of a lesson. Often all this requires is introducing a task which students can solve on their own and which does not require constant teacher attention. In the case of 10a this was, as we saw, a longer period during which they were working on their own. I subsequently found it useful to think of lessons I had to teach almost entirely in terms of tasks that would require some form of student activity.

Breathing space, ie removing the pressure of the situation, is also needed when things are heating up in a conflict. I found Hargreaves' notion of 'non-punitive exile' useful. It can help to send a disruptive pupil out of the classroom for a while, in order to give him/her time to calm down and break the cycle of escalation. The pupil can then be asked back in after a few minutes. It should be made clear from the beginning that no punishment is intended.

4 Flexibility

A better way out of a cycle of confrontation is restructuring the situation in such a way that this cycle can be left without the teacher appearing to retreat. Being able to change course, being able to give a situation a new turn that is unexpected for the class can be an immediate solution for discipline problems. Hargreaves (1972) advises 'introducing a new twist into a situation' as a vital skill in dealing with discipline problems. Burghardt (1987) in an article for language teachers advises beginners to watch out for signs of boredom and fatigue and act on them early by introducing a new activity. One example of how a situation could be given a different turn is the episode *Ghostwriters* which initially looked as if it only allowed for two alternatives: putting up with the cheating or ending up in the role of detective. Turning confrontation away from me succeeded because in making it clear to the students that justice in this case could not be entirely my responsibility I had restructured the situation.

A second example is the episode with the sentence that I split up into 33 words. It is doubtful whether this was very useful in terms of language-teaching aims, but it saved my day. Literally my day, because if that lesson had gone wrong, it might have affected all the subsequent ones. Reacting to fatigue by flexibly adjusting the lesson can prevent disciplinary problems from happening. I found that a lot of my problems went away as soon as I was able to see what the situation was, take a brief pause for reflection and then replan and improvise on the basis of my assessment of the current mood and/or the physical state of my class.

There are several reasons why being flexible is difficult for a beginning teacher. One reason may be that he/she has planned the lesson so well that no deviations from the lesson plan seem possible. Teacher training may partly be at the root of this problem. My training, for instance, had to a great extent been about executing lesson plans which had to be handed in to the tutor beforehand. Of course, it is both necessary and useful to learn how to plan a lesson in minute detail. Yet as we saw in Chapter 1 (in the section about uncertainty) the teaching situation constantly makes it imperative for the teacher to be flexible because plans crumble under suddenly changed conditions: it may be minor oversights like a page reference, as in the episode *A harmless question*, it may be a fire alarm, a class test in the lesson before or a helicopter landing outside the window. This is not to say that preparation is superfluous. Lessons should have a clear structure. But this structure should – wherever possible – be open to student contributions. Well-planned and at the same time well-taught lessons often have a clearly structured phase at the beginning to give orientation and security (see Chapter 7). The plan for the remainder of the lesson might then include alternatives and variations. It might give teacher and class some leeway as to how much should be covered by the end. The best lessons I taught were usually those in which I had indeed invested a fair amount of preparation. My plan, however, was often adapted, varied or discarded during the actual lesson because of student contributions.

Flexibility is not only needed in planning but also in reacting to potentially difficult situations. One particular noteworthy form of doing so is what Hargreaves (1972) calls 'humorous decontamination'. It means giving a potentially threatening situation a twist to the humorous. This can often prevent confrontation. Hardly any handbook on teaching practice fails to mention humour. Yet dealing with a class situation in a humorous way is something personal. Humour is no technique. Solutions and ideas have to arise – as in many other cases (see Chapter 7, p125, *Silences*) – from the situation and on the spot. Trying to define humour on paper may well destroy what it is all about. However, the point cannot be made too strongly that humour is essential to the students, although it should never be at their expense.

Being in a classroom together with children and adolescents has frequently left me with situations bordering on the bizarre, surreal and sometimes absurd. I often found humour to be the only humane way out. 'Can we have more of these laughing moments?' one student wrote in his course evaluation. In one of the previous lessons I had not been able to resist the temptation of putting together – for the purpose of a dictation – two lesson texts, one about the *Titanic* and one about a school outing. The text for the dictation ended up being a rather bizarre story in which a school bus collided with an iceberg. When I first read out the dictation as a whole the class's reaction was wild laughter. I had immediate doubts. Would they not treat it as a joke and therefore perform badly? In the event, the results of the test were very good. When handing back the papers I asked the class why they had done so well. They said one reason was that the text had been so funny. Having listened to it, the test no longer seemed like a test but rather like a relaxed practice session. Teaching young people, it was said in Chapter 1, is often loaded with emotions. Humour – not irony or cynicism – is often the best way of coping with emotionally charged situations.

Good lessons, for me, alternate between humour and seriousness. It is the teacher's art to balance the two against each other, by allowing the situation to go to the limits of control in one phase and retrieving it in the next. Drawing the borders between such different phases within the rhythm of a lesson can be a problem. It helps to make it clear to a class when the change from a humorous phase to serious business has to be made. This can be done by commenting on both unrest and the need to be quiet again and, if necessary, by insisting. A good example of how classroom control was sustained within a very relaxed lesson and of how some of the points just made have become part of the personal style of a teacher can be found in a study of a ceramics class in Eisner (1979). What emerges from the description is a teacher who is able to notice sources of potential problems early and defuse them with humour. Mr Gebhardt, the teacher, is able to strike the right balance between freedom and humour on the one hand and control and seriousness on the other:

> Mr Gebhart's humor is not that of a stand up comic. Rather, he has a subtle whimsy with which he defuses potentially tense situations ... [On one occasion] a student responded to an order with 'What are you? A dictator?' Without hesitation, Mr Gebhardt responded 'I'm training to be one. This is the first step.' The girl laughed and the problem was solved. (Catford 1979 p322)

Part Two
Change

Chapter 3 **A different angle: humanism**

Diary
....

20th October

Their surprise seemed genuine

Went to school this morning with several escalation scenarios on my mind: If they do X, my retribution will be Y, etc. I was going to activate those scenarios the moment anyone dared disturb my lesson. The lesson passed in utter peace. Was it that they had sensed that this time I was prepared to go all the way? Maybe. There was a second reason. The class did, at one point, become slightly restive. On impulse I asked them if the noise and their talking were directed against me. They said 'no'. Their surprise seemed genuine.

5th November

Who has read the novel?

Advanced class (Catcher in the Rye, first lesson). Catastrophe. I was not well enough prepared. I go through a rather forced routine of comprehension questions. A lot of silence. At one point I am so fed up that I break off the lesson and ask them why things are going so badly. More silence. I ask who has read the novel. Sylvia says she has. But only the first chapter. She did not get anything out of it. Why this slang? Stupid book. I tell her the book was supposed to be appealing to young people; that's why it was on the reading list. It wasn't appealing to her. One or two others disagree. They liked the slang. Some first impressions of the book are reported. Sylvia's being so outspoken has cleared the air. At least this is better than the blackboard rituals before, when I was answering my own questions. I still feel I have to defend the book and wonder how I will survive the next couple of weeks.

20th November

Why do teachers always feel they have to defend themselves?

Ann came for a reference today. She has left our school and the dreaded 10a to do an apprenticeship. It is strange, she says, how little interest she had in English while she was at school and how important it has become since. She wants to work abroad. We talk about how we experienced the last two years.

One thing she does not understand: Why do teachers always feel they have to defend themselves? I tell her to picture herself in front of 30-odd people. Discipline in my lessons, she says, had not been as bad as I thought. At least there had been worse. The part she had disliked most were the lab lessons. The tapes had been too difficult, the whole exercise seemed pointless. And another thing: the times they had really hated me were not those little skirmishes about opening windows, but when I had compared them to other classes and, like all my other colleagues, told them how much better these other classes were.

18th December

Borrowed voice

Something nice happened in yesterday's lesson. It is hard to capture in words and it is even more surprising that it happened. I wanted to have a feedback session about an essay they had written. I had first meant to ask students to read out their own work. I was going to take notes while they were reading it and then point out some of their mistakes. However, in the event, I decided to read some essays to the class myself. Before I read them, I said correctness of language would be no issue today, because I would read out the texts in a corrected version. While reading, I aimed for the tone of voice in which I would usually read out a text written by a native speaker or a literary text. My purpose behind this was the following: as the content of the essays (it had been a comment on a short story about school life) was of a more personal nature than what the students usually had to write for their English lessons, I did not want to use my command of the language for evaluating the correctness of what they had written. Instead I wanted as it were to 'lend' my voice and command of the language to a linguistically imperfect text and to transform it into something more authentic. It is difficult to pin down any hard and fast results of such a procedure, but the change in atmosphere as well as the temporary change in my role were noticeable. Suddenly I was no longer the marker who watched out for mistakes and meted out penalties in red ink, but rather someone like an editor who tried to make sense of what they had written and who explained and defended the text when it was queried by the class.

10th January

Michael

Tried a similar procedure in 11c today and read out a passage of student writing.[1] I read it in a completely neutral tone of voice, correct sentences as well as incorrect ones. Students were to write down the correct version. I started to dictate sentences from Michael's text. He took exception, saying the others would laugh at his mistakes. I only just persuaded him. In the event the others found some of his mistakes but accepted a lot of the others as correct. After the exercise he looked satisfied. He had seen that the majority of the class would have made the same mistakes.

---

1 Technique taken from Rinvolucri (1984 p 89).

16th October

Their first test

11d. I give them back their first test. I go in with the pile of test books feeling I have been too lenient. But I can tell from their faces how much difference the good results have made for them.

12th January

The teacher shows interest

Detail: Andreas leans back and yawns. I ask him if he is tired or exhausted from listening to English. I do so without any intention of calling him to order. He immediately assumes this is a reprimand and is about to defend himself, assuming that if the teacher shows interest in him it can only be for disciplinary reasons.

13th January

Did the right thing

I was lucky and did the right thing. Richard (17) came in late during the first lesson. He put his head on the table and was about to nod off. I fight off the instinct to tell him off or fire the first question at him. In the second half of the double period he says that he has woken up and now takes an active part in the lesson.

25th March

An Italian class

Several of us teachers are attending an Italian class a colleague teaches. After the lesson, Ralph, who was sitting next to me, said it had been a long time since he last experienced a lesson from a pupil's perspective. Pupil conversation during the lesson, we agreed, was less disruptive than it would have seemed to us had we been standing in front. We probably would not have tolerated it if we had been teaching. Yet we had to admit that despite all the talking the lesson was still clearly comprehensible to us.

16th April

An essay

I set grade 9 an essay. Is it worth learning foreign languages? Are we learning the right ones considering the fact that, for instance, Turkish is the most frequently spoken foreign language in our country? I am interested in the subject, so I decide to sit down at my desk and write the essay as well. Good fun. But it teaches me how much hard work it is to write anything coherent in 90 minutes by hand and without the possibility of editing and drafting.

17th April

They were quite critical

They read their essays to the class today. I was about to move on to something new when they remembered I had written something, too. So I read what I had written. They were quite critical. I should have stuck more to the topic. Afterwards I wondered whether it would undermine my authority.

5th May

I showed them English tea

Today's lesson in grade 5 did not go particularly well. Until one of the kids in the first row of seats saw the thermos in my briefcase and asked what was in it. I said tea. English tea? In fact, it was. With milk in it. Ugh. Was I serious? I said I was and promised to show it to them after we had finished our exercise. Then I went round with a plastic cup of demonstration liquid. The lesson came alive.

20th May

Irate farmer

Grade 11. The unit in the book is about dialects. There are a few recordings on the cassette that goes with the book. They have listened to these already. At one point I tell them a story about how I got chased from a field by an irate farmer when walking on the Pennine Way. I try to say what he had said, imitating his local accent. At first they cannot understand it, but in a sudden burst of interest they ask for repetitions and explanations. I write some expressions on the blackboard. Then I have them guess the dialect version of words they know. What caught their attention seems to be the tinge of reality that had suddenly come into the classroom. Last year I had them spend a lot of time on authentic listening materials in the lab. There appears to be a more basic aspect to authenticity: a piece of language became real in today's lesson because I had experienced it myself and stood there as living proof of it.

15th June

Crankshaft

In one of today's lessons the word crankshaft came up. I asked – not really expecting an answer – if anybody could explain what it was. Marc, who never gets his tenses right, could. He patiently answered all the questions I had to ask, because it took me so long to understand. Correcting his English will never be the same again.

20th June

Jens

Decided to test some of the pupils individually. Jens was an obvious candidate. We had had a little show-down at the beginning of the year when I told him either to take part in the lesson or to leave the room. He never said a word in class again. Now I had to assess his spoken English. In his interview this afternoon, Jens suddenly began to speak in fluent English. He told me that he had been to the US several times. I resisted the urge to ask why he had never told me his English was so good.

25th June

It gets on my nerves

About half the advanced course (17- to 18-year-olds) is giggling as I come in. They have done so rather often during the last few weeks. Today they just can't stop. I try to take it in my stride and for the first fifteen minutes I react with humour. They still do not calm down. Then I tell them how much it gets on my nerves and threaten to go on strike. They stop it.

30th June

No need to calm them down

The end of the school year is approaching fast, we have finished the book and are reading short stories now. I had given the class an option: they could either write an essay or perform one scene of the story for the class. In today's lesson two pupils take the stage. There are two roles in the scene. One is that of a headmaster. It involves long passages. The other is that of a schoolboy. It is only a few lines. There is utter concentration and attention during the play. No need to calm them down. The performance is followed by a lively discussion about the quality of the acting and how this is to be assessed because the roles differ so much in length.

9th September

Contents table

We started work on the textbook. The book (a reader) has enough material to last us through the year. I had a number of texts in mind that have worked well in the past and for which I had worked out lesson plans. Mainly because I wanted some variation I asked them to turn to the contents table of the book, have a look at it and tell me what texts they were interested in. They came up with a number of stories and a text about jazz music, none of which I would have chosen because to me they did not seem the right material for a well-structured lesson. We decided to begin with a short story and then move on to a text about blues music.

10th September

Their own story

Important lesson in grade 11. We went through a second short story. I had been about to set them a comprehension question for the next day. This would have been quite adequate, because they need the practice and could have based their answers on the book. Instead I asked them to write their own story. The results were read in class today. Many of them were full of mistakes. I chose not to correct them at this stage. Some of the stories were both original and good. Their authors must have put a lot of work into them.

3rd February

Trust

Advanced class today. I put down a piece of chalk and tell them to write down the lines of the Shakespeare chorus we recited yesterday. They hesitate a long time. Lars and Gregor crack a few jokes. It makes me angry but I am trying to remain quiet. Then I make the task somewhat easier. I write down the beginning and the end of the first line:

Two households .... dignity

After a long time Tanja asks what they are supposed to do. She goes to the blackboard and fills in 'both alike in', underlining what she has written with the chalk on her thumb. Slowly things begin to move. I try to send out signals that I trust them and that I assume they basically want the same thing as me. Afterwards the lesson goes better.

4th February

Quiet 'revolution'

It is not until the end of the second part of the lesson that I decide to go ahead with a long-contemplated and quiet 'revolution'. I tell them they are free to come or go for the next couple of weeks. They listen indifferently. Tanja frowns. I don't know if I have made the right decision.

5th February

New freedom

Yesterday, despite their new freedom, they all came for the early lesson … and yawned.

6th February

Tom

Tom's parents have split up. He has left home. The next thing he wants to leave is school. It is his second attempt to pass the exam. He only wants the piece of paper and then to get on with his life.

9th April

Project week

The school is having a project week at the end of the year. I wonder why it is always at the end of the school year, when everybody is tired, that new forms of teaching are given a chance. Still, it seems worth a try. Like anything in a school with 1200 kids it takes weeks to organize. The admin work that goes with it, ie channelling the entire school into projects, preferably the ones of their choice, checking lists, and chasing up individuals, is considerable. For those who have to do it the actual teaching becomes a marginal aspect of the job alongside all the other tasks.

5th July

The bell has become superfluous

Project week has started. School has, for three rare days, transformed itself. Classrooms have become workshops. There is the constant hum of activity rather than the successions of relative silence and deafening noise in the corridors. Pupils simply carry on with what they are doing whether someone is standing over them or not. The theatre people rehearse in the entrance hall. The bell has become superfluous. The staffroom is open. Right now it is no longer a sanctuary with a lock. None is needed.

Analysis

Introduction

Classroom control is an essential first step. However, it is not an end in itself, as quotes like 'We don't mind if you don't teach them anything as long as you have control' might suggest. Once control has been achieved there is still the question to answer: control for what? Establishing control with the help of some of the age-old tricks of the trade is a temporary measure. This chapter is an attempt to go 'beyond control'. As the title of this chapter suggests, its aim is to see classroom interaction from a different angle. The chapter is about occasions of learning – my learning from both the situation and the students. This was not a process of a linear ascent, but rather a bumpy shuttle between failure and sudden insight.

What did my insights consist of? Above all they were the beginning of a new perspective on students, their personalities, opinions and histories. They meant a new perspective on Jens, the discipline problem who turned out to be a fluent speaker. 'Don't try to be their friend,' had been the advice. Yet there seemed to be a point in meeting students outside the classroom situation I had defined so narrowly in my own terms. By and by, I got a better understanding of students. This, in turn, led to more security and made me less obsessed with control. Rather it enabled me to look at events that could not be foreseen (as in the episode *A harmless question* in Chapter 2) no longer as a threat but to respond to them flexibly. I started to react to surprises with surprises. All this amounted to an approach that was slowly going beyond the advice given in the previous chapter. Understanding students' personalities and motives might initially have been little more than a technique to gain control in the classroom. However, the episodes in the first part of this chapter show that it also led to changes in my relationship with the class. The episodes about Andreas who yawned or Richard who fell asleep are instances when I spontaneously decided to do without preventive action and when I found that, despite what the books said, such non-intervention was actually successful. Similarly I could see that changing my approach to students' mistakes could make a difference in atmosphere, as in the episode *Borrowed voice*. The atmosphere in the classroom was something I was becoming more and more aware of. One important ingredient of it was the role I chose for myself. On one or two occasions I could see what a difference it made when I talked about my own personal experience and stopped being spokesman for the book. This nearly always caught students' attention. It was as if they could sense within seconds that I was leaving the teacher's role (see the episodes *I showed them English tea* and *Irate farmer*).

I have selected the above episodes with three concepts in mind. Each of these concepts stands for a certain attitude in personal relations between teachers and their students. The concepts go back to the theoretical framework of Rogers' client-centred therapy in which he has outlined the conditions necessary for a client to change in therapy. Rogers (1990 [1967] p305) assumes that similar conditions apply in the classroom. Since Rogers' work is part of the humanistic movement in psychology, approaches to education and language teaching basing themselves on findings from humanistic psychology will be referred to under the label 'humanistic' or 'humanism' in this book. One basic assumption of humanistic education is that learning is 'facilitated' not so much through teaching skills but rather through certain 'attitudinal qualities that exist in the personal *relationship*' (his italics) between the teacher and the students (Rogers 1990 [1967] p305). There is some empirical evidence to show that these attitudinal qualities make a difference to learning (eg the study by Klyne 1972). The most frequently mentioned of these attitudes are:

1 Empathic understanding: '... the teacher has the ability to understand the student's reactions from the inside, has a sensitive awareness of the way the process of education and learning seems *to the student*' (his italics) (Rogers 1990 [1967] p310)

2 Valuing (other terms are 'prizing', 'acceptance', 'trust' and 'unconditional positive regard'): 'It is caring for the learner, but a nonpossessive caring. It is an acceptance of this other individual as a separate person, having worth in her own right. It is a basic trust – a belief that this other person is somehow fundamentally trustworthy.' (Rogers 1990 [1967] pp308–9)

3 Realness: '... the teacher can be a real person in her relationship with her students. She can be enthusiastic, can be bored, can be interested in students, can be angry, can be sensitive and sympathetic. Because she accepts these feelings as her own, she has no need to impose them on her students ... Thus she is a person to her students, not a faceless embodiment of a curricular requirement nor a sterile tube through which knowledge is passed from one generation to the next.' (Rogers 1990 [1967] p306)

4 Autonomy: One important consequence that follows from understanding and valuing students is that they are trusted – at least to some extent – to know what they need. Understanding and respecting students therefore means respecting their autonomy and leaving important decisions about the learning process to them.

It is one thing advocating empathic understanding, valuing, realness and autonomy in the therapeutic field where client and counsellor meet voluntarily. Applying these principles in an educational context is another. Curran (1972 p128; pp193–4) claims there is in principle no difference between therapy and education. Rogers is more cautious and hopes that these attitudes '*may* [his italics] exist in the countless interpersonal interactions between the teacher and pupils' (Rogers 1990 [1967] p305). So, how applicable and useful are empathic understanding, valuing, realness and autonomy within an institution like a school? I shall try to explore this question by looking at three aspects:

1 As a first step (*'arguments'*) I will make a case for their usefulness at school and especially in language teaching.
2 Secondly, I will look at potential *obstacles* school might put in their way.
3 Finally, I will suggest a number of *practical steps* that can be taken to foster these attitudes.

To bring together what is said about the four concepts I will analyse a piece of student writing and try to sketch how student work in foreign languages can be looked at from 'a different angle'.

1 Empathic understanding

Arguments

Children live in a conceptual world that is not immediately accessible to adults. They need a lot of intensive listening – done by the teacher. To give but one example of such conceptual differences: one colleague who taught maths put a problem to 11-year-olds. He did so in writing using the expression '*Gesichtspunkte*', which as a lexical item in German means *aspects*. Taken completely literally it can also be understood as *freckles* (literally 'dots on the face'). It was exactly this literal meaning that conjured up the image of a freckled face for many of the children in the class and therefore made any understanding of the mathematical problem they had been set impossible.

As far as language teaching is concerned the additional point should be made that empathy is credited with playing a decisive role in the acquisition of a foreign language. In various studies (eg Guiora 1975) empathy has been shown to influence language learning. It is certainly open to discussion whether empathy as an attitude can be learnt, especially at school. However, classes will no doubt benefit if attitudes like empathy are not only discussed in the classroom but brought to life by the teacher.

The most fundamental case for empathic understanding has, in my view, been made by Buber (Buber's work *I and Thou* [1937] and his notion of the 'encounter' of persons have influenced Rogers). In a famous speech about education (*Über das Erzieherische* [1925]) Buber explores the nature of education in terms that bear a clear resemblance to empathy. Empathy is seen in connection with the powers teachers have over children. What constitutes the attitude of the educator, what gives legitimacy to his/her efforts, is the ability to 'experience the other side'. Educational influence – and, after all, educators are the persons who have chosen as a profession to effect, through their person, changes in other persons – runs the constant risk of degenerating into an imposition of will by the educator. One safeguard against such an arbitrary imposition of will exists if educational decisions are based on the needs of the child and if the power educators are endowed with is exclusively used for the benefit of those educated. Otherwise there is a danger that education bases itself on the preconceptions of those who educate and not on the reality of those who are being educated. For this purpose, educators have to be aware of the effects of what they do on their pupils. It is therefore essential for the educator not just to have thought about the other side or imagined it – but to have experienced and felt what it is like being on the receiving end.

Obstacles

Teachers are not famous for being good listeners. The reasons for this lie in the situation described in Chapter 1. One of my older colleagues said that the strain of the job for him consisted in constantly being in a position of having to 'offer' something and in having to keep the show moving. It may be for this reason that teachers tend to interpret a moment of silence that comes up in a class discussion or a conversation as an invitation, if not a request, to say something and fill this silence with talk. In both classes and parents' evenings I have seen teachers making their speeches and hardly even bothering to ask for comments. If they did, they hardly allowed enough time for anyone to speak out. Rather they used silences – which might well have been pauses for reflection and the preparation of a speech by one of the listeners – as an opportunity for making yet another speech themselves. This tendency to talk rather than to listen is all the more regrettable, since the isolation of the work situation in the classroom makes it necessary to get as much feedback from students as possible. How can teachers avail themselves of this feedback? What can empathic understanding mean in the classroom?

Suggestions for empathy

Listening to students

One first step is simply – although it is far from simple – to listen to students. Since listening can be difficult with thirty people in a classroom, asking students to make personal statements might be of help (see the episodes *My ideal school day* in Chapter 4 and *Career in English* in Chapter 5). Equally, a different seating arrangement in the classroom, like, for instance, a circle, may help to make listening easier for the teacher.

In a different frame

A second step may be to talk to students outside the frame of the teaching situation. This was the case in the episodes *Jens* and *Why do teachers always feel they have to defend themselves?* in this chapter. Many students react to the alienation described in Chapter 1 by, as one student wrote, 'putting up a wall around myself, so that school can't educate me any more'. When talking to Jens on a face-to-face basis it was possible to look through a gap in this wall. Students may of course want to stay behind their protective wall. This has to be respected. However useful it may be to leave the framework of the teaching situation, it should be clear that problems of relationship that arise within the formal teaching situation have ultimately to be resolved within that situation.

Ask them

'Ask them' is one of the maxims Brandes and Ginnis (1986 p121) advocate for student-centred learning. It means that teachers should not take decisions on their own but ask students for their opinions. 'Ask them' stuck in my mind as a maxim for the classroom. On many occasions it has served me as a reminder that it might be worth at least asking students for their opinion. In the episode *Their surprise seemed genuine*, 'asking them' whether their behaviour was directed against me did turn out to be a surprising success. I had taken the class's behaviour as a genuine provocation and was about to react with sanctions. My question came quite unexpectedly for them. I had asked it in genuine interest. The class said 'no', no provocation had been meant. After this the situation was defused. It had been possible to talk about the situation and step outside the framework set by the institution. I, myself, could no longer impose any sanctions because I knew about the group's good intentions. Conversely the group had, by saying they did not mean any provocation, almost entered into something like a contract to be co-operative for the rest of the lesson.

Written feedback

It was probably after occasions like these that I decided to give student opinion a more regular hearing. One method of doing this that worked quite effectively in my classes was getting written feedback on my teaching at regular intervals. The answers such evaluations produced are part of Chapter 4.

Teachers as learners

One final and very obvious step language teachers can take to experience what it is like being on the other side is becoming a learner again and putting themselves through the experience of learning an unknown language. In my case the languages were Italian and Chinese. The 'Chinese experience' will be referred to in the diary section of the next chapter.

2 Valuing

Arguments

Practically every educational reformer has made a case for valuing and respecting children. In the case of the '*Reform*' movement (see Scheibe 1969 for general educational aspects and Howatt 1984 pp169–91 for its impact on language teaching) this took place at the turn of the century against a background of schooling which in many cases could hardly be called humane. Berthold Otto, one of the leading proponents of the *Reform,* criticized 'adult arrogance' and demanded that adults 'stop seeing children as merely "stupid little creatures" who still had a lot to learn' (quoted from Scheibe 1977 [1969] p87, my translation). He demanded that children be taken seriously and respected as human beings.

Adolescence may be 'a long dark tunnel'; on the other hand it does not last forever. It was helpful for me to meet students after they had left school, as I did in the case of Ann. I could see how sensible the one-time antagonists had become. This does little to solve current problems, but trying to see the virtual adult in a child or adolescent helps to put these problems into perspective.

Obstacles

Some of the criticism made by the *Reform* is still valid today, although it is important not to paint too black a picture. Connell (1985), for instance, notes specifically the extent to which teachers do actually care about their students. On the other hand there are innumerable accounts which indicate that respect towards students is something not necessarily to be taken for granted in schools. 'Unconditional positive regard' is still no natural ingredient of the school classroom. On the contrary, there is rather a lot of conditional regard around at schools, ie regard that is conditional on how well a child does in terms of grades and achievements. Note the profound effect of the good grades I almost didn't give in the episode *Their first test.* Encounters between a teacher and a class are about evaluation almost from the word go. What should be mere feedback on the learning process for both teacher and students is routinely used as an instrument to assess students. Nor does the need to control classes help much to develop a caring attitude. Confrontations arise when teachers try to enforce discipline. As a reaction teachers feel the need to ensure that the difference in status between them and the students is made clear.

Such situations are of course prone to fostering attitudes in teachers that tend to see students as inferior partners. Caring and valuing is therefore a very ambitious objective in a school environment. A more realistic aim may be respect. Respect for others is taken for granted in adult life. At school and with children it is – still – a different matter. School teachers do not teach adults but those who are younger, less experienced, less competent, etc; there is a temptation to mistake a difference of age for one of value. One student, writing about herself as a pupil, stressed that she had never been good at English and that there had only been one single teacher in her career who, despite her being a failure at English, had given her the feeling that he respected her all the same.

The following is a list of minimal steps towards valuing.

Suggestions for valuing

Appreciation of student work

School is centred around the evaluation of student work. Looking at such work from a different angle can be a point of departure. This is made easier when the work is the result of an individual effort containing something only one particular student can do or express. This is especially true for drama and essay work. Since language teaching revolves around finding and scoring mistakes, an important step towards valuing students in language classes is to look at their work from a qualitative point of view, ie trying to see what is special and unique about a particular achievement. This is not to say that evaluation of student work should be dropped altogether, but an occasional change in attitude can do a lot to put some of the quantitative and often only seemingly objective data about students into a broader perspective. Being non-evaluating, ie looking for quality rather than quantity, resembles what Eisner (1979) calls 'connoisseurship' or 'educational appreciation'. An example of what this could mean for looking at student work in English will be given at the end of this chapter.

Respect

A second step has already been mentioned. It is keeping achievement and the person of the student apart. The statement of the pupil referred to above suffices to show how necessary this is. Robertson (1989 [1981]) writes that in dealing with disciplinary matters rules of respect should still be observed. The measures taken should, if at all possible, be presented as necessary for maintaining conditions that enable the class to work. They should not appear to be directed against an individual. This is, of course, difficult when everybody is tense and angry. In view of the next principle, 'realness', it may even sometimes be better to be open about negative feelings rather than to pretend to be effecting emotionally neutral crisis management.

Students' expertise in other subjects

It helps to value and respect students if not only their work but also they themselves are occasionally seen from a different angle. One possibility is showing an interest in how a student does in other subjects. He/she may be bad at English but brilliant at science. Acknowledging such expertise and keeping it at the back of one's mind can mark a change of attitude towards a student (see the episode *Crankshaft*). Again, this applies particularly to languages, where success is seen by many as being dependent on a special gift.

Rigorous caring

Finally, it is no prerequisite for valuing that a teacher be a believer in humanistic schools of thought. What is decisive is rather that he/she cares. Students are well aware of this. One grade 11, for instance, were quite critical about the emphasis one of their past English teachers had put on grammar and the meticulousness with which she had gone through every single chapter of the grammar book. What they deeply respected and appreciated, however, was that their teacher was committed to what she did and that she would not stop until everybody in the group had understood a grammatical rule. This attitude seemed by far to outbalance the rigour of her lessons.

3 Realness

Arguments

For Rogers the 'realness' of the teacher is the most basic condition for learning to take place. It is the absence of a real person in front of the class that is often criticized by students. The following statement is taken from a public letter a group of school leavers wrote to one of their teachers:

> We have certainly profited from your knowledge and your clearly structured lessons. Yet although you have presented to us your view of the world, we have never got to know you as a person.

The fact that knowledge is often presented in schools in an impersonal way, ie 'faceless' and through a 'sterile tube', is also noted in classroom observations. Wesemann reports:

> It is all the more astonishing that the vast majority of the observed teachers showed an attitude of neutral reservation towards the subject they taught, so that their 'educational history', ie the history of what the topic had once done to them, was entirely ignored. Teachers tried to tease out structures, to explain phenomena, to interpret metaphors, but they did not tell anything about themselves. It was almost as if they were afraid of disclosing something about themselves ... (Wesemann 1984 p85)

These two statements support Rogers' claim that realness is fundamental. It is fundamental to teaching in yet another way. Realness refers, above all, to emotions. As we have seen, 'real' teachers can be 'enthusiastic, can be bored, can be interested in students, can be angry, can be sensitive and sympathetic ...' (Rogers 1990 [1967] p306). If Connell (1985, Chapter 1) is right and emotions are not just an initial barrier to teaching but the very substance of it, realness touches on a core aspect of teachers' work.

Finally, as an aside: I had colleagues who were, to put it mildly, idiosyncratic in their attitudes and methods. They were criticized for this. At the same time, ex-students, looking back on one of these colleagues, acknowledged how much he had influenced them. Much as he might have antagonized sections of the student population he had converted a considerable number of his students to actually studying his subject. Not because his methods were brilliant or student-centred. Quite the contrary. It was because, as one of his students later said, he was living his subject and, at the age of 55, was enthusiastic about it to the point of being obsessed. It was this and the fact that in teaching he was being himself that seems to have made the difference. It cannot be overlooked that in doing so a lot of things went wrong. Nor would I want to make a case for being fanatic about a subject. Yet what he taught has stood the test of time.

Obstacles

Being real with regard to one's emotions entails risks. This is true for students as well as for teachers. It is one thing taking such a risks on a one-to-one basis. Taking them in front of a group whose benevolence is far from guaranteed is another. There are plausible reasons for teachers wanting to wear masks (see Chapter 2). Indeed, it looks as if many teachers shy away from the 'immense strain' it involves 'if you care at all about what you're doing' (see p15) – probably not because they lack responsibility but rather because they can only bear so much exposure, vulnerability and emotional strain. It almost seems like a natural defence mechanism for them to distance themselves from their classes and from what they do. Moreover, there is, if a teacher chooses to be open to his/her class, a very real risk of going to the opposite extreme and getting carried away on an ego-trip. How, then, can the risks of being real be borne?

Suggestions for being real

The positive as well as the negative

Realness involves, according to Rogers, accepting the positive as well as the negative. There has been considerable irritation about humanistic approaches because of maxims like 'accentuate the positive' which were, especially in the work of Moskowitz (1978), given a very prominent status. For the sake of honesty and 'realness', negative aspects of personal relationships (and, after all, the first chapter shows that life in the classroom can be full of these) should be acknowledged, too. I have included the episode *It gets on my nerves* as one example to show that being humanistic is not exclusively about smiling at students.

Something of your own

As a teacher I often had the impression that, whatever exercises I could devise, the ones in the book were better. Textbooks often have an aura of perfection. And why shouldn't they? They are in all senses of the word finished products. A lot of expertise has gone into their production. And yet it seems sad if there is no room for teacher creativity. One obvious step towards realness is therefore not to rely entirely on ready-made published material. Of course, such decisions have to be taken within reason and within the very narrow limits of the time available. On the other hand, although there may be no point in reinventing the wheel, there are reasonable compromises.

Time permitting it is well worth considering working with 'home-made' materials. A lot of teachers do so anyway, and there are fundamental arguments in favour of it. It may be debatable whether preparing, for example, a newspaper text for use in teaching (glossary, numbering lines, etc) is an efficient way of using preparation time, because such a text can often only be used once or twice. On the other hand, teacher-made materials can have a more profound effect on classes than published materials, because they actually encapsulate the teacher's thinking and the learning effort which went into their preparation. This process will have changed the teacher – maybe only to a minute degree – but the likelihood is that such change will communicate itself to the class.

Authenticity has for a long time been a buzzword in language teaching. It usually means using written or spoken texts not specifically designed for language teaching. Such material can be very stimulating. At the same time it should not be forgotten that there is another aspect of authenticity: the realness of the teacher. Such real-ness displays itself in the teacher's relationship to what he/she teaches. Often it is small things like objects that make the difference and personalize lessons. Where I work there has been a tendency to teach beginners' classes more and more with the help of overhead transparencies, because it is easier to portray 'authentic' situations outside the classroom in this way. It should not be forgotten that what is presented is only an image of reality. There is a lot to be said for time-honoured practices like bringing a box of objects into a beginners' class. The speech function presented by asking 'What is this?' and at the same time pointing to a toy car on the table may not be very authentic; on the other hand, children who acquire their first language spend a lot of time doing exactly the same. More importantly, objects are something personal and unique between the teacher and the class. I decided, for instance, to present most of the dialogues in the beginners' book with the help of two hand puppets who, although far from authentic, quickly became the trade mark of my English lessons. More about them in Chapter 7 (see the section *Lively dialogues: Tony and Ilona*).

Stories

Taped materials are authentic in the sense that they can display features of spontaneous speech not always available to the non-native teacher. On the other hand, there is nothing like a story told well and told 'live' by the teacher. Such a story may go back to a teacher's personal experience (see the episode *Irate farmer*). Admittedly, there is a risk here of becoming self-indulgent. Yet student evalua-tions show again and again how deep an impression anecdotes about personal experience in the target culture leave. Research studies (Labov 1972) have been undertaken to analyse the role of storytelling in our daily lives. It has been shown how important the 'oral' rendering of experience is. There may therefore be more to storytelling than meets the eye.

Morgan and Rinvolucri (1983) have done the profession a great favour with their collection of story skeletons. The teacher memorizes them and then uses them for a free rendering of the story to the class. Telling a story freely almost automatically means the storyteller is emotionally involved, more so in any case than in reading out something or playing a tape. Usually an element of acting out the story simply 'happens', when, at the climax of the story, the vital bunch of keys is dropped or the photograph on which the plot of the story hinges can suddenly be 'seen' by everybody on the classroom wall, although the teacher is only pointing to an empty spot. The devices for good storytelling are very simple. Telling a story to a class also means being in contact with the class. It means eye contact and, not least, a high degree of concentrated listening on the part of the class. Storytelling is a two-way process. There is constant feedback on how well the story and the language are being understood. The language of the story (unlike that of a recording) can be varied, simplified, repeated, made more juicy as the teller goes along and takes in the reactions of the audience. Difficulties in comprehension can be addressed on the spot in this way. Finally, and maybe most importantly, instead of an image there is a 'real' three-dimensional person standing in front of the group.

This is not to say that the use of films, videos and tape-recordings does not have a firm and undisputed place in language-teaching. For one thing, showing a film may provide the teacher with the much needed breathing space argued for in the previous chapter. (Showing a film may even be a way out of momentary conflict, although I believe this is only a short-term solution.) And watching a film need not mean the class remains inactive. There are now sensible suggestions as to how to use film and video as a means of activating students (cf Cooper *et al.* 1991). By the same token, showing the film version of a novel that has been read in class is a useful back-up for comprehension, comparison, an introduction to film language, etc. Electronic media are part of children's 'reality' of life and school education has to respond to this.

However, responding to this cannot simply mean replicating in the classroom the rather dubious practice of media consumption that takes place outside school. There are more and more complaints by teachers and parents that children can no longer concentrate and listen without talking or doing something else at the same time. This seems hardly surprising when children grow up in an environment where the TV set has become a background noise like that of an electric fan. The effects of children's constant exposure to electronic media are profound. One fundamental consequence may well be that, since the world is increasingly experienced via representations and images, it is harder and harder for children to see anything real and to tell the difference between reality and representation. This is particularly worrying with regard to images of violence. The world, as it presents itself to young people, is something completed. It is cast in concrete. There is little that can be done to it. It is therefore not surprising that apathy, boredom and a feeling of being neither in charge nor responsible can prevail among students. It is doubtful whether the answer to such a situation is to bring even more media into the classroom. This may well amount to entering a race that cannot be won. Instead, one thing school can do, and should do, is (in a very literal sense) to bring reality back to the classroom.

4 Autonomy

Arguments

Wesemann (1984 p81) has observed how students can be genuinely curious about a subject. For instance, when they were helping to clear away demonstration objects from the lesson, they showed interest in the things standing around in the biology store room. However, as soon as these things became part of the machinery of a lesson, the children's interest vanished. Children are inherently interested in the world and want to learn about it. The development of a small child and the way it conquers the world until formal instruction sets in bears witness to this. It is therefore one of the central tenets of humanistic education that learners have to be given freedom if learning is to take place. Lewin (writing in the thirties) shows the connection between freedom and learning:

> Only in a sufficiently free life-space in which the child has the possibility of choosing his goals according to his own needs and in which, at the same time, he fully experiences the objectively conditioned difficulties in the attainment of the goal, can a clear level of reality be formed, only thus can the ability for responsible decision develop. (Lewin 1935 p179)

Freedom is one of the most fundamental values in humanistic psychology. It bases itself on existentialist thought for which freedom is not a theoretical concept but something that has to be experienced and lived (eg Warnock 1970 p2). Humanistic psychology criticizes behaviourism and Freudian psychoanalysis for seeing clients as determined by stimuli or drives and not crediting them with free will. Goldstein (1940), one of the founding fathers of humanistic psychology, argued against Freudian drives and assumed an innate tendency for growth in humans, ie a quest for new experiences. Reports about therapy conducted within the framework of humanistic psychology frequently refer to moments of freedom and choice.

Numerous cases have since been made for 'free schools' and 'free education'. It was notably authors coming from the background of humanistic psychology who were very critical of state school education and therefore advocated more freedom in education (for instance, Rogers, Goodman or Maslow). Radical school critics have influenced a whole generation of teachers who were educated in the sixties and seventies. Lines between educational camps are still drawn according to what stance teachers take on the freedom and autonomy of learners. To some the 'freedom to learn' may appear as an issue of the sixties and seventies, and they therefore approach it with scepticism. Admittedly, the practice that followed from radical ideas has not always worked as well as was originally hoped. Yet if children are to take over responsibility for what happens in the world they should be prepared and educated for it. If a society is to be free, if it is to be run and governed by responsible persons, such responsibility has to be practised and learnt. It has to be learnt by doing and by making mistakes as well as by seeing successes. Democracy cannot begin and end outside the school gate.

Going back to psychology and even philosophy and looking at ideals like autonomy and freedom, as I have just done, may seem to be going rather far afield for a practitioner. I would argue that practical action is, in the long run, not only influenced by the demands of the situation, but also by beliefs or ideals. Ideals may be far away from everyday staffroom discussion, it may indeed be a certain violation of decorum to voice them among colleagues. All the same it is ideas which provide the motivation, the source of energy, the stamina for a teacher to go on with his/her style of teaching in everyday life.

Obstacles

Looking at everyday life, the amount of freedom that should be granted to children during their education has always been the subject of heated controversy. The call for freedom rings alarm bells for many school teachers, because their day-to-day work shows them that the very opposite is true: when teaching children and adolescents nothing happens without control. It should indeed not be overlooked that a lot of the work done on learner autonomy has been done with a view to adult learners. So age is a factor not to be neglected when considering giving autonomy to learners. The age groups I teach range from 10 to 19. Autonomy will mean something different for each of these age groups (see also the remarks on 'free will and its problems' in Chapter 4). There are strands of the *Reform* movement like Steiner education that strongly advocate the autonomy of schools. At the same time, they only grant a very limited amount of freedom to younger students, because they think this is not appropriate at their age.

The suggestions I am going to make in the following sections will in all likelihood not go far enough for radical critics of the school system. And there is no denying that I have taken a pragmatic stance by limiting the discussion to a few first steps towards autonomy that might not be too risky to take. On the other hand, these little steps might have a cumulative effect.

Suggestions for autonomy

Giving orientation

In Chapter 2 I quoted a teacher who began her lesson by giving students some idea of what was going to happen in the lesson. It can be argued that although it is only the teacher's plan that is made public, even this affords a small measure of autonomy to learners. It is a gesture of respect and care, showing that the teacher has thought in advance about what he/she wants the class to do. I have found it to be a simple device to signal to the class that I assume they have an interest in the aims of the lesson and do not just want to sit back and let it happen. It also makes me more accountable for what I am doing. In some lessons I write a short list of items I want to cover on the blackboard. At certain intervals I briefly point to the blackboard and tell the class which part of the programme we have arrived at.

Choice of texts

One criticism of language classes is that they are too tightly planned and often prestructured by the materials used. While accepting that there is often a need for this, especially when teaching beginners, it is worth looking at how rigid planning can become more flexible. Some decisions and actions may need the expertise of the teacher, while others may not. Collections of texts which are often used for advanced classes lend themselves to giving students some choice because the texts are not graded. When I gave students a choice in the episode *Contents table* the texts they selected were completely different from those I would have chosen. Since the students' choice was not guided by pedagogic criteria, the texts were difficult to teach. This, however, was offset by higher student interest which kept the lessons moving.

I used a similar procedure in a more systematic way when preparing a longer reading project. The idea behind it was that the energy and the will to read a longer text will be increased if students have a say in deciding what they are going to read. This is, in any case, what motivates 'authentic' reading outside the classroom. Before reading a longer novel with an upper intermediate class, I therefore brought with me photocopies from every tenth page of the novel and handed out these copies to the class. I told the class they should imagine they were in a bookshop and only had ten minutes to leaf through the book. The copies were assumed to be the pages they had, by chance, turned to. They were to read the pages they got, then pass them on and, in a 'conveyor-belt' fashion, receive another page from their neighbour. Afterwards they were to try as a group to bring together as much information about the book as possible. Using this information, we would decide whether we would 'buy' the book, ie whether we would read it in class. This task made the class read with intense concentration. The pupils took the task seriously, because its outcome would have consequences for what we were going to do in future lessons.

Participation in running classes

Students can be involved in running a class. In grade 7 I often started lessons by asking pupils to translate a few lexical items. Gradually students took over this phase. I was surprised at how much fun they got out of running this small part of the lesson, eg when they had thought up tricky forms of irregular verbs or when they tested their mates with a thoroughness I would not have dared to apply myself. Martin (1986) has developed a method called 'Learning by Teaching' which systematically hands over teaching functions to students (see also Martin 1985 and Graef 1990).

Handing over responsibility

Sharing responsibilities can have an unburdening effect for the teacher. The *Ghostwriters* episode in Chapter 2 is an illustration of how a problem became a group matter. Handing over responsibility to students can not only be of help with problems of assessment and discipline, it can also show the way out of deadlocks in classroom interaction, although it may look like the harder option initially. Brandes and Ginnis make a distinction between 'rescue' and 'support':

> Handing over responsibility to students requires them to be confident enough to accept it. In order to build this confidence, the teacher will need to avoid rescuing them every time the going gets a bit rough. (Brandes and Ginnis 1986 p54)

If the teacher always 'rescues' a classroom discussion, because he/she is afraid of silence, students will 'know that if they wait long enough they will be rescued eventually, so why should they bother to take the risk and volunteer?' (Brandes and Ginnis 1986 p55). When responsibilities are more equally distributed, there is a possibility that it can become clear to both teacher and class what a teacher can sensibly be expected to be responsible for. It should be noted, however, that, at least from the students' point of view, the line between a teacher who hands over responsibility and one who does not care is very thin.

Project work

Projects are a way of handing over responsibility to students and therefore of making them more autonomous. The *Project week* mentioned earlier made a considerable difference in terms of atmosphere and student motivation. Its main feature was that the compartmentalization of the school day into subject slots had been suspended and that students worked on one project or theme for a longer period of time. This goes some way towards addressing the criticism that the experience children are subjected to at secondary school is – because of the structure of the timetable and the lack of co-ordination between the different subjects – essentially a fragmented one. The point not to be overlooked here is, of course, that the creation of freedom and the involvement of learners is not only a matter of steps taken by individual teachers in individual lessons. Learner autonomy is a matter of how teaching is organized as a whole. Teachers can find individual solutions to problems arising from the necessity to control. Ultimately, however, certain problems, like the fragmentation of school knowledge and the lack of motivation it can produce, will only be resolved if schools are organized in a different way. It is here that the limits of innovation from below are visible. Again, it should be noted that many proponents of humanistic education are arguing for free schools.

One example of how schools can be organized in a different way is Steiner education, which gives, for instance, great priority to a holistic syllabus. Subjects are taught in 'blocks', ie they are allocated a large number of hours per week for a certain time, after which another block takes over. Approaches of this kind have been advocated as being conducive to language learning (Schiffler 1989 p137). Putting them into practice requires a lot of organization and the co-operation of the school as a whole. This may be beyond the scope of the individual teacher. Which is not to say that it is impossible. Legutke (1988) reports on several projects that made use of the fact that English as an international language is present in the students' immediate environment. One language project he describes involves a class interviewing international passengers at an airport (Legutke and Thomas 1991 pp157–256). Projects like this may be too labour-intensive for the teacher to be adopted for regular teaching. However, there are other, more manageable alternatives. And, more importantly, it is desirable for a class to have in the course of a school year at least one classroom experience that is unlike the others and unique. School theatre work is the most common example of such an extraordinary event. It has a lot of unused potential for language teaching.

Projects result in a product. This product belongs to those who produced it. It has been observed that students are more motivated when, at the end of their learning, there is a product they can identify with (Wesemann 1984 p112). This is particularly true of art lessons. It will be argued in a later part of the book that certain forms of essay writing may have this effect. Essay writing means more autonomy, because the product belongs to the students. They have invested their work in it and therefore identify with it.

Evaluations

A further step towards student autonomy is asking them to evaluate lessons. Stevick (1980) introduces this as the riskiest of seven steps towards being 'humanistic'. Students 'are free to talk openly about their reactions to the course and to the language; about what works for them and what doesn't; about what delights them and what bores them; how they feel about the language and the people who speak it ...' (Stevick 1980 p30).

I first used student evaluations because I wanted information about how a certain type of exercise had been received (see Chapter 4). Since the process of evaluating these exercises proved to be as interesting as the exercises themselves, I asked students for evaluations of lessons at regular intervals. I tried not to use them as a reaction to crisis, but only when I felt confident enough to bear and respond to criticism. The procedure I used was: I wrote a number of questions on the black-board (or sometimes just a plus for what they liked and a minus for what they disliked) and asked students to take a piece of paper and write down what they thought of their English lessons. These evaluations were written anonymously. When everybody had finished, the papers were folded and each student 'drew' someone else's statement. The class sat in a circle and students read out the paper they had drawn. The evaluations were discussed. I just listened. Often such sessions were a relief, because my perception had been dominated by a lesson that had not gone well, whereas students were much more positive than I would have thought. The evaluations also counterbalanced the opinions of the more vocal members of the class, because the 'silent majority' had their say. There were also surprises when exercises I thought had been wonderful, because there had been so much action in the classroom, turned out not to have been popular at all. Student evaluations will be described and discussed in detail in Chapter 4.

In conclusion

Buber (1925) argues that freedom is a necessary condition for education, but that it is not in itself education. For him, freedom is the potential to commit oneself. For the teacher this means that granting freedom cannot just mean standing aside and opting out of the proceedings. The same goes for those being educated. Freedom means responsibility, as the section *Handing over responsibility* above tried to demonstrate. Brandes and Ginnis talk of a group 'owning' their learning, meaning that they both possess it and have responsibility for it (Brandes and Ginnis 1986 p26). Ownership is not necessarily easy. One of my students wrote about the greater responsibilities given to her during the final two years at school:

'At the end of the day you yourself have to know how much you have to learn in order to reach your goals. This is not that easy.'

The vital conditions for freedom and autonomy to succeed are the attitudes described earlier. Only if the risks and difficulties of freedom are faced in the right climate, ie not in one of indifference, only if those who are given autonomy and those who hand it over trust each other is there a chance that – as O'Neill (1991) wrote – student autonomy will not become student neglect.

5 Steffen's essay

The following is an example of how the principles outlined in this chapter can be brought to bear on language teaching. The example I have chosen is a piece of student writing, Steffen's essay. It is an autobiographical reflection. I will use the essay to make the following points:

1 The essay is an example of the difficulties advanced students face when trying to express something that is important to them.
2 Discussing the essay is an attempt to move from evaluation towards appreciation (cf Eisner 1979). In order to give substance to my appreciation an outline of the formal and aesthetic qualities of the essay will be given.
3 The content of the essay reflects some of the themes discussed in this chapter. Because in all likelihood Steffen has never had any exposure to humanistic theories, it shows that the issues raised in humanistic education and psychology have some reality for students.
4 The essay shows how an activity like writing, looked at in terms of student autonomy and self-reflection, develops an educational momentum of its own.

Steffen's essay is reprinted here in its original form, without any corrections.

'I can remember that I always did like and wanted entering school, and it was only allowed, though I was five, because of that. And I think nothing or not much had changed all my school time. Entering the grammar-school was also my own, actually non-influenced – by parents or teachers –, decision. In the 9th form, I could not have reached the 'aim of the class' and another time I decided otherwise the advice of my teachers and my parents.

All my school time I wasn't ever an excellent pupil, but in the first years, I think, a good one, although I was a mix of 'Michel of Loneberga' and 'Rocky'. eg. one time it was offered to me a long extra-holiday (four weeks), because in one of my, in that time often and typical for my, 'fits of rage', I had hit my teacher with hard long wooden stick (cudgel) and had beaten an other pupils teeth out.

It is interessting for myself that I was getting more and more, not phlegmatical but quiet and more introversive but my notes were getting worser.

I don't know, if it is a merit of the school that I'm were getting so, maybe, or maybe not. It was a developing of myself, perhabs.

School had learnt me many interessting and more less interessting things, especially since 10th form, but I regret, she had not learnt me enough for life. Maybe she was not strong enough, she had not demanded enough.

I ever had problems in languages, particularly with our own, German.

In former times I was not able to speak and write it in a right way (rightly).

I was called legasthenic, and following this, all the time at school and after school I have more or less difficulties to express (articulate) myself in words or in speaking. I think, mainly caused of this I was getting more quiet — I was insecure of myself — maybe.

School did not learn me to overcome this completely.

As another problem I regard, that school do not or is not able to do, form the pupil characters and support their inclinations and talents (enough).

I for myself, when I had to choose the subjects, which I wanted to do for my examination, could not decided me for long time. I had known only two-three subjects, which I had favorized. I had taken then the subjects not following my notes, but my interesst.

In spite of all bad experiences and opinions about school, it was a nice time, and had I known this already at school I had considered school as a spare-time (wörtlich! [German for 'literally' J.A.]) before life goes on, although I had known she was not the good preparator for life.'

Usually, when student work is quoted in a book for teachers, a 'good' example is given in order to show what can be done. Steffen's essay is no such example. Its language and spelling are anything but flawless. I am devoting a section to this piece of work because I think it shows the dilemma that students in advanced classes find themselves in. It is, in his case, one between the complexity ('depth', see Chapter 4) of the message he wishes to convey on the one hand, and the limitations of his language on the other. There are two ways of looking at this piece of work: marking it for correctness or appreciating it. Let us start with what language teachers normally do: mark it. Taking into account the number of mistakes and the length of the text, the potential mark this piece of work would get is not very satisfactory. In fact, it is quite likely a fail. This view is easy to corroborate:

The writer gets many basics wrong: use of pronouns (*school – she*), wrong morphology (*worser, he do not, I'm were*) plus various spelling mistakes (*interessting*). He uses a large number of literal translations from German: *to decide me – 'mich entscheiden', notes – 'Noten'* (for grades), *learn me* for *teach me*, etc. Many words only appear in approximations, ie the author has no clear mastery of the lexical items he uses. Examples are *introversive, phlegmatical, favorized* and *caused of this* for *because of this*. The facts are clear enough. The language is, by any standard, unsatisfactory.

On the other hand, if I suspend for a moment my marking criteria I enjoyed (and still enjoy) reading this particular piece of work. The language may sound odd, but what he has to say, ie his themes, are interesting. Not only that, it is also the attitude he conveys and the way the contents are structured which reveal that the author is trying to give shape to his experience, making the best use of the language at his disposal.

In writing about how school affected his own development Steffen – although he probably never had any exposure to such themes – comes up with the now familiar themes of humanism and humanistic education. Here are two examples:

[Entering grammar school] *'was my own, actually non-influenced by parents or teachers-, decision.'*

'I don't know, if it is a merit of the school that I'm were getting so ...'

In both sentences Steffen describes a moment of freedom and choice in his life, contrasting it with the possibility of being determined by his education. He goes on to look at school in terms of the contribution it made, or didn't make, to his self-actualization:

'... school do not or is not able to do, form the pupil characters and support their inclinations and talents (enough).'

How are these themes given shape? How are they developed rhetorically? The text changes between general statements about the writer's development (*'I wasn't ever an excellent pupil'*) and individual episodes to illustrate these statements (the *'long extra-holiday'*). The point of the narrative is to explain the author's present attitude and character. The story unfolds in a well-crafted pattern. The first two paragraphs span part of the author's school career. In the third and fourth paragraph he steps back (*'it is interessting for myself ...'*) and looks at himself. He then turns to the subject of languages, his difficulties with them and how these difficulties explain what (he thinks) has become of him. (*'I think, mainly caused of this I was getting more quiet'*). He uses a certain pattern in his writing: a thesis is followed up with an example. The thesis that school does not form pupils' characters is illustrated by the difficulties he had in choosing the right course. He ends by summing up his verdict. Looking at the way Steffen makes his point it becomes obvious that, despite his insufficient command of the language, he tries to use various structuring and rhetorical devices including an attempt at self-irony in the second paragraph. However, his attempts at self-expression run into difficulties with the foreign language and he has to be quite inventive to resolve these difficulties. It is particularly his attitude of detachment and reflectiveness that takes him to the limits of his syntax, because the syntactic structure of his paragraphs and sentences mirrors his attitude and therefore has to accommodate all kinds of caveats. One example of how he tries to solve these complexities is the overlong participial construction *'actually non-influenced by parents or teachers'*; another one is all the little clauses spliced into his text: *'though I was five'*; *'but in the first years, I think, a good one, although ...'*.

Drawing together these observations we arrive at the following dichotomy: on the one hand the author clearly has difficulties with many of the basics of the language; on the other hand the message he wants to convey, if he is given the freedom to express what he wants, is of considerable complexity. My first impulse was to tell him he should go back and sort out the basics and until then go for a lower level of complexity. Yet a closer look at the examples just mentioned shows that he is quite resourceful in trying to express himself and in finding a way around these basic problems. Steffen's case is that of a student who is prepared to use written communication as a way of expressing himself. Steffen was, incidentally, a very good art student and was therefore probably good at devoting a lot of time to the 'crafting' of a piece of work.

Steffen's essay essentially reads like an attempt to overcome the difficulties of expression he mentions in his biographical statement. So he cannot go back in time and pretend he is a beginner again. Too many expressions and skills belonging to an adult mode of expression are already at his disposal: abstraction, elaboration, irony together with some adult vocabulary. What can be done? Remedial work would not be easy. It would have to be done at different levels. One level would quite simply be basic grammar and morphology. It would probably be best for him to do this on his own, maybe going over some chapters of a beginners' book again. This, however, would only be part of the task. Another task would be to make him aware of the coinages he uses, like *developing*. Yet another step would be to show him the true linguistic complexity of what he attempts to express, maybe by showing him what his sentences would be like in correct English. Working from this, intermediate versions could perhaps be found in which complex sentences would be broken down into smaller units. Chapter 4 will show how important an attitude of realism is for advanced learners. This would indeed be an important aim for Steffen.

All this requires time and individual attention. It would require a lot of rethinking as far as the organization of classes was concerned because it goes beyond the usual format of written work (write homework, teacher corrects homework, homework is given back). In his case several rewrites would be necessary. There were other students in his group who had similar problems. However, these problems were not the same for each individual student. If anything was really to be done about their problems, the approach would have to be individualized. This means that advanced remedial work in a group with students of this kind probably does not benefit much from the usual second and third run through 'the most important' chapters of grammar, because difficulties of expression are too individualized by this stage. The task of doing something about them is probably best tackled in the kind of workshop atmosphere which is so familiar in art lessons and so alien to language lessons.

Chapter 4 **Depth**

Diary

30th August

A number of books

Came back from my summer holiday with a number of books bought in Britain: Maley and Duff's Drama Techniques, Frank and Rinvolucri's 'Grammar in Action', Morgan and Rinvolucri's 'Once upon a Time' and Moskowitz's 'Caring and Sharing in the Foreign Language Class'. Each book is a collection of exercises. They are like various scenarios specifying the number of actors, props, space, plot, time, etc. The scenarios should translate easily into lessons.

5th September

My ideal school day

First lesson in 11c. Tonia, Anselm and Leo are not there. It is exceptionally peaceful. This helps me to decide to try out one of the exercises from the books I bought. It is 'My ideal school day' from the Moskowitz book. I tell the class to take a piece of paper and write down what their ideal school day would be like. After ten minutes they are to read what they have written to the group. At first the situation is somewhat confused, because they do not know what to write. Silke asks if this is one of my experiments. Tina asks whether they are to write something serious or just fantasies. There is a noticeably different quality to the lesson. It makes a difference that I have left the decision about what to say to them. Before they read out what they have written I ask them to move the desks to the wall and sit in a circle.

I had originally felt uneasy about moving the chairs into one circle. It would be noisy on the uncarpeted floors. Colleagues understandably do not like this. The class is not entirely enthusiastic about it, either. Moving furniture means physical work and this is not in keeping with a certain ethos of inertia in the older classes. Together with the tables goes a sort of safety barrier. The truce ('Leave me alone and I will leave your lesson alone') between teacher and back rows of seats has been broken. Nor does the classroom necessarily become a nicer place. The middle of the room is suddenly transformed into an empty expanse with papers scattered all over it. My open style of teaching begins with a firm invitation to clear the classroom floor of debris. Not the best of starts with 17-year-olds.

In the event, rearranging the classroom is a relatively smooth operation. I had been afraid of noise and chaos which would give away my subversive methods. These fears are unfounded, probably because I start by explaining that tables and chairs should be carried and not dragged. It takes some insisting to ensure that there is only one circle and no second row of seats. As I have no table I put my papers on the floor in front of me. It is a bit like a theatre rehearsal.

I leave it to them who wants to report to the class as a whole. No reaction. Then one student who is good at English begins. What he says is definitely on the safe side. Some terribly polite jokes about school. After the lesson he complains that there has been no correction. On the other hand, by and by a lot of them do speak English – maybe out of sheer surprise. During the time when I am standing aside they are actually working on the task. Only when I get back into a normal teacher-centred lesson does the conversation lapse back to the normal routine of me asking questions, calling on someone to answer and getting a very defensive reply or no reply at all.

22nd September

Hotel receptionist

One student is to play the role of a tourist in a foreign country. He/she does not know the language and can therefore only communicate through mime. The group sit in a semi-circle and act the part of a hotel receptionist asking yes/no questions. The tourist is given requests like 'I don't like the picture of the flying geese in our room, could you exchange it?'[2] The guest has to convey his/her request by non-verbal means. The group must co-operate to help.

I ask for a volunteer. With Marc I am very lucky. He doesn't usually say much during lessons but this time, quite to everybody's surprise, he immediately throws himself into the act, using powerful body language taken from comics. Every now and again he stands helplessly in front of the group, who are supposed to assist him. They are enthused by his gift for mime and forget to ask more questions. It takes them a long time to understand that it is they who have to take the initiative. At first they look to me, waiting for a cue to speak. I force myself not to react with leadership. Instead I gesture towards Marc, signalling to them that he is their partner and not me.

The exercise produces a lot of mime and fun. Unfortunately not much language. When students get involved, their questions are often completely elliptic. In the end Marc gets applause, something that has not happened to anybody in the class before.

5th October

Object story

This week we did 'Object story'.[3] The class is split into groups of three or four. The groups sit in a circle around a chair. Each member of the group puts a personal object on the chair. The task is: they are to assume that the four objects belong to one person who has gone missing. The objects have subsequently been found. They are like a trail the missing person has left behind. The group is to construct a story that explains what happened to the assumed owner. Having done this they put the objects back into a plastic bag and exchange their bags with other groups. A new round of story invention begins. In the end, all stories are reported to the class and compared.

---

2 Taken from the exercise in Maley and Duff 1982 pp125–6.
3 cf the exercise 'The envelope' in Maley and Duff 1982 pp135–6.

The exercise went down well. Better than previous ones. Probably because its content was less serious than in the exercise 'My ideal school day'. Again: productiveness in terms of language seems dubious. Most stories are conceived in German. One competent member of the group translates it into English. On the other hand, Michael makes a long and well-crafted speech. He has not said so much in one coherent chunk of speech in the entire year.

The difference the exercise makes is that the objects introduce something personal. One group makes a story about four cigarette lighters. Michael says that he was grateful for the additional preparation time the groupwork had given him. For once there had not been others who were quicker than him.

6th October

Good for busy teachers

The exercises are good for busy teachers. I can leaf through the books and will be able to 'stage' what I have read the next morning. In many cases no further material has to be prepared. Each exercise generates an activity lasting between 20 minutes and a whole lesson. Little preparation is required. Almost all the work invested is recyclable, ie if I have to learn to tell a story as a lead-in to an exercise, this story can be used many more times. It becomes part of a repertoire of 'materials' that need no photocopier in order to be distributed to a class.

Moreover, the exercises fit flexibly into my lessons. The advanced classes which last 90 minutes need breaking up in any case. The exercises are a good opportunity to do this.

7th October

Post mortem 'Object story' 11c

What has gone wrong? The afternoon lesson was not the right time. I came in rather nervously and reacted to their questions with impatience. I felt under attack too quickly. I had the impression that when I told them we were going to do another of 'the exercises' it meant for them that the actual teaching had finished. Of course, this was partly due to what I had said at the beginning of the lesson, when I asked them not to sabotage what we were going to do. Then (again!) I did not leave them enough time, so that I got nervous about that too. I did not quite know what to expect at the end of the lesson. This time they were speaking German most of the time in their groups.

13th October

Real phone number

In the beginners' class we were doing numbers from one to nine. The pupils read out groups of figures I had written on the blackboard. We then went on to telephone numbers. At one point I asked them to dictate their own phone number to someone standing at the blackboard. It is hard to describe, but looking at the faces and seeing the mixture of concentration and suspense it was apparent that dictating their own real phone number did make a vital difference to students.

23rd October

Claudia

During break I talk to Claudia. She takes exception to being cast in the role of an 'intellectual' just because she does not like playing games in class. In any case, after twelve years of being dependent on teachers' questions, to her the task of being creative seems to come a bit late.

25th October

Work experience[4]

I go in and ask them whether they have ever worked for money during the school holidays. All of them nod. Mild interest. I tell them the story of how I spent two summers in an office earning money as a student and about how boring and alienating it had been. Afterwards I split them up into pairs and ask them to tell each other stories about experiences at work. After twenty minutes of animated discussion they report back to the group and, after initially very short comments, a lively discussion about school in comparison to professional life follows. (Many of their peers who left school earlier are by now earning their own money.)

The good atmosphere somehow transferred itself to the rest of the lesson. It had been a good start and so the following part of the lesson on grammar went well too. In fact, it seemed as if after this 'free' activity at the beginning the rather tightly structured grammar work I followed it up with was more welcome than usual.

14th December

One-word dialogues

Did 'One-word dialogues'.[5] Groups of four are set the following task. Two of them are to communicate in a dialogue. They are only allowed to ask or answer with one word. Behind them there are two 'secretaries' who write down the dialogue. After the dialogue is finished the script of the dialogue is read out. The two speakers give their interpretation.

The exercise half works and half does not. A number of well motivated students do the exercise and apparently enjoy it. I take part in one of those groups, although I hadn't intended to, in order to make up numbers, and this way I find out how difficult the exercise actually is. Feel rather disheartened.

The less motivated students give the exercise a twist to make it fit their needs. For them my lessons apparently often consist of class discussions that go lame and end up with me asking questions. They see these discussions as a sort of evasion game. You score a point if you say very little, ie if you get away with a one-word answer to one of my questions. This game is also played when we do this new type of exercise. Some of the players try to be utterly monosyllabic. The funny thing about the one-word dialogues is that it asks for exactly the thing which is usually 'forbidden': being monosyllabic.[6] The results of the class's

---

4 For a similar exercise, see Morgan and Rinvolucri 1983 pp96–7.
5 Maley and Duff 1982 (1978) p113.
6 A similar principle is used in Morgan and Rinvolucri's 'Revenge questions' (1983 p13).

efforts are rather absurd dialogues which cannot be explained to anybody. Mario, however, takes the exercise seriously and there is a sense of modern drama to the dialogue he made up with his partner.

19th December

Shifting furniture

Tina comes to me at the end of the lesson saying my classes are all about shifting furniture. This is what she is going to remember. I don't know what to say. Thinking about it later, Tina's statement sounds more positive than it had in class. Yes, moving the tables takes time and persuasion. At the same time it is a powerful symbol, at least to me, of the fact that something can be changed in the classroom, even if it is just the way the tables are arranged.

In fact, they have changed more than that. The climate in the classroom is now different. At least occasionally. Every now and then the role I play as a teacher differs from what it usually is. The 'frontal' situation is taken away from me for part of the lesson. I step back and become an occasional supplier of language. When groups and pairs report back to the class I can again behave differently. Students talk about personal experience. They express opinions. They tell stories. What they say is no longer answers that can be either right or wrong. I have to listen, but listening has become easier. Even the fact that the students and I are physically sitting on the same level (today on the floor) helps, because I am nearer the student who is speaking. At the same time there is no constant need to evaluate what students say. In fact, I quickly learn that if I refrain (against all my teacher's instincts) from commenting on student utterances it actually helps the discussion. There may be embarrassing silences at the beginning, but if I can bring myself to bear them, in half the cases students take over. If it gets off the ground, the discussion has a momentum of its own and is no longer a centrally controlled process. This in turn means less pressure for me to react to every-thing that is said. It seems most natural for me to make my own contribution at the end when the group have had their say. In the second half of today's exercise, however, I ended up being very firm with Tina and her neighbour in order to ensure there was silence for someone who wanted to speak.

5th January

Education otherwise

Text: 'Education otherwise', about parents who don't send their children to school but teach them at home. It is one of the rare occasions when Volker, who has more or less been ignoring the lessons over the last few weeks, shows an interest, because it is his situation that the text is about: not being able or prepared to cope with state school education, not being able to operate under the rules.

16th March

If I hadn't made him speak

Autonomy: Mario (17) never speaks English unless he is made to and put on the spot. Today he has something to say that clearly is important to him. He starts in English, gets stuck and then wants to go on in German. I insist that he tries in

English. He says he doesn't know the English word for the German 'Regierung'. Or rather he knows that he knows it, but now he needs it, it's gone. I tell him what it is. He is annoyed. He has heard it so many times before, has read it, maybe has even used it in a translation. But now in the actual situation when he needs it, it simply is not there. Noticing this is, as he readily admits, a new insight for him. He says he has suddenly realized that there is a difference between recognizing the word 'government' in the book and being able to use it. He is all the more shocked since this applies to such a basic word. He wouldn't have found out about this, he adds, if I hadn't made him speak.

1st April

Chinese intensive course

I am going to take the role of a student for the next few days. This is day one. The teacher turned spectator: I am very disappointed when I don't get a turn to say something because the teacher has decided the exercise is taking too long. As a teacher I would have done the same. As a student I'm addicted to praise. My fears: being called on to say something, mistakes, corrections, irony, ridicule. I keep comparing myself to the others. Even more important for my well-being than I thought: comprehension of what is said in class.

2nd April

Outside the teacher's field of vision

I didn't get a chance to speak for an entire 90 minutes because I was sitting outside the teacher's field of vision. She never once moved during the lesson. It takes her ages to find the right place on the tape. Worse still, while playing the tape she does other admin tasks, like sorting out papers, which makes me feel I am just plugged in and then left on my own. The group had no control over the tape. It would have been so easy to have given it to us.

Over lunch we were cooking a Chinese meal. We were to speak only Chinese. I saw little use in speaking the language to others who speak the language as badly as I do. I want a native speaker to listen to me.

3rd April

A good teacher

Today the joy of being taught by a good teacher. At no point does any boredom creep in. It just doesn't. Maybe this is what good teaching does to you. It leaves you with a feeling of having spent an agreeable morning that has passed quickly. Interestingly, C, the teacher, uses basically the same method for about four hours. Nor is there a lot of variation in terms of the material he uses. It is probably his flexibility. There is something improvised and at the same time secure about his lessons. He departs from the dialogues, makes us re-enact them, picks out difficult bits and goes over them again with a different twist to them. He makes me surprised about myself: about how much Chinese comes out of me. Occasionally he talks about our difficulties. He asks whether we take in what others say in class (which is exactly what I find difficult). Are we able, if it is someone else's turn to do an oral exercise, to keep one step ahead? His interest in our answers seems genuine. It makes me want to tell him my story. He says we should, at least occasionally, say something that is true and not only make up answers the content of which does not matter to us. Don't say something just for the sake of having spoken the language. Everybody gets their turn. He knows when to call on someone. He answers questions, but also knows when to stop before his answers get too long. When I give my talk the next morning he says it is too short. This won't do. Something I haven't been told in a long time.

4th April

Waiting for the break

As a teacher I often dread the sound of the bell which puts a premature end to my lesson plans. As a student I'm craving for the end of the lesson, when regimentation ends and I can speak to the others in the group. I am reminded of how important the interaction taking place during break time must be for my students back at school. At the moment I, too, am waiting for the break, pretending to take notes but actually looking at my watch or out of the window at two house fronts.

Analysis

Introduction

Chapter 3 started out from classroom situations that made me change some of my attitudes towards students and teaching. What I described were mainly reactions to incidents during lessons. This chapter goes one step further. It is no longer about reactions but about interventions. Its focus is on method.

With freedom and autonomy at the forefront, many humanistic authors consider teaching methods as secondary. Brandes and Ginnis (1986) put a quote by Rogers at the beginning of their book: 'I know I cannot teach anyone anything, I can only provide an environment in which he can learn.' They go on to make a distinction between 'didactic' and 'participatory' (Brandes and Ginnis 1986 p17) methods, a juxtaposition in which 'didactic' stands for conventional teaching, which is seen as something that should become obsolete. 'One of our own favourite maxims is "a good teacher soon renders herself obsolete".' (Brandes and Ginnis 1986 p19.) On the other hand, if learners are to exercise their freedom, this freedom has to be such that they can use it. It is here that both teacher and method re-enter the scene. Teacher control and method need not be in conflict with student autonomy. Stevick (1980 p25) points out that teachers can prepare and control their lessons in such a way that student initiative is possible. In fact, he claims that if control is skilfully exercised, this will provide the best opportunities for student initiative. The following chapters are intended to show how the attitudes described in Chapter 3 can inspire the methods used in the language classroom (see Chapters 5–7) and, conversely, how a particular method can create an environment conducive to these attitudes. The latter point is the subject of this chapter, which proceeds as follows:

Section 1, *Depth and needs,* starts out from observations I made as a student on the intensive course in Chinese mentioned in the diary section. It identifies students' personal needs as crucial factors in the success of a lesson. The term 'depth' (Stevick 1976) is introduced to describe how language and classroom proceedings interact with these personal needs.

Section 2, *From the communicative approach to humanistic exercises,* examines to what extent the communicative approach to language teaching takes care of student needs and depth. A new type of exercise (new for me!) is presented, which I used in my classes. The episodes *Hotel receptionist, Object story* and *Work experience* in the diary section are examples of this approach. I will use the term 'humanistic' for this type of exercise.

Section 3, which forms the core of this chapter, analyses student reactions to 'humanistic exercises' and describes the *students' needs* implied by their comments. A categorization of these needs is attempted.

1 Depth and needs

When attending the intensive course in spoken Chinese I described in the diary section I experienced a teacher whose style, probably without him being aware of it, exemplified some of the attitudes described in the previous chapter. What did he do? The teacher was obviously a good listener (*His interest seems genuine*). What was more, he was au fait with what was happening 'out there' in the classroom. He was aware of our difficulties and seemed to know what was on our minds. He saw when we were getting tired and asked 'Do you manage to keep one step ahead when others are doing an exercise?' He managed to see our needs at almost every moment of the lesson. These needs are hinted at in the episode *Outside the teacher's field of vision*: eg my wish to say something, my need for attention and not to be left alone with the tape recorder, my need for esteem when comparing myself to the group, and my need for praise. Other teachers on the course were less perceptive. In their lessons unfulfilled needs often turned into fears: fears of not understanding, being laughed at, being corrected, etc. Our teacher made sure there was no fear for me in his class. And he made sure there was no boredom, either. Why? Because what we did and what we said – especially the true statements he encouraged us to make – mattered. They mattered more than the repetition of phrases from dialogues we had done in other lessons.

The observations I have just described are summarized by Stevick's term 'depth'. The term is taken from research into verbal memory. In a study by Craik *et al.* (1972) subjects were given lists of words to remember. They were then asked different types of questions, one about each word. Some questions, it was claimed, made them extract more meaning from the word on the list than others, eg a question like 'Does the word fit in the following sentence?' requires the subject to extract more meaning from the word than the question 'Is the word written in capital letters?' Questions of the first type are said to call for a processing at greater 'cognitive depth'. It was found in subsequent recognition and recall tasks that words processed at a deeper level were dramatically better retained in memory. These findings show that the 'deeper' a word is processed, ie the more meaning it has for someone, the better it is remembered.[7] In the original study the meaning of a word was defined in terms of the information it carried. Stevick has expanded the scope of what an expression means to include *what it means to its speaker*, ie the feelings, memories, personal experience associated with it. The meaning of 'depth' in Stevick's sense goes beyond cognitive depth and includes 'the entire personality of the learner' (Stevick 1976 p32). It refers to the connection of a language item 'with our plans, with our most important memories, and with our needs' (Stevick 1976 p36). It includes particularly the affective. Depth is the difference that saying a sentence makes to the speaker.

An illustration: I have, in my repertoire of English expressions, the sentence *They took everything they could lay their hands on*. In my memory the expression is linked to an evening in Bellingham youth hostel in Northumberland. I can, even though it is almost 20 years ago, still picture the situation. It was cold, and we

---

7 Stevick (1990) has subsequently pointed out that there is evidence that contradicts this claim and that depth may therefore be misleading as a metaphor. However, even though the term may not hold in terms of experimental evidence, the wider meaning Stevick has given to it still seems valid for me.

were sitting round the fire. My English was not very good, so I was trying to listen to the conversation. And suddenly I understood this expression which was the equivalent of the German, '*Was ihnen in die Hände fiel.*' I thought it would be something useful to know in the future to show how idiomatic my English was. I have hardly used the expression in the past 20 years. Yet its depth, ie the evening and the sudden joy of having understood, made both the episode and the language stick in my memory. What happened to me points in the same direction as the evidence quoted by Stevick: language items of personal significance, especially if they arouse emotions, stand a better chance of retention in the memory.

Personal significance is not only a matter of what language is presented but also one of how it is presented. 'Depth' in its wider sense also refers to the 'here and now'[8] of the classroom. 'Depth' is the personal significance to the learner of what happens there. It 'refers to what difference participation in a given activity – drill, dialog or Spanish Club picnic – makes to an individual, relative to his or her entire range of drives and needs' (Stevick 1976 p47). Does the activity make the learner afraid? Does it take care of his/her need for security, esteem or appreciation? The depth of a word, an exercise, pairwork, an exchange with the teacher is the extent to which it matters to the learner in terms of his/her personal needs.

This 'range of drives and needs' which is captured in the notion of depth has been the subject of psychological study. It was described by Maslow (1987 [1954]) in his well-known hierarchy of needs. His analysis of motivation shows that humans experience needs on several levels. Whenever one level of needs is satisfied, others of a higher order appear. At the base of the hierarchy are 'deficiency needs' starting with physical needs like that for food, shelter, etc, moving 'up' to the need for security, belonging, esteem. Beyond the satisfaction of basic needs there are 'being values' or 'growth needs' which include wholeness, perfection, fulfilment, justice, richness, simplicity, beauty ... At the top of this pyramid of needs there is self-realization: the need and the capacity of a person to live to his/her full potential. Conversely, needs of a higher level are of little relevance if the ones below them in the pyramid have not yet been fulfilled.

Many diary entries in Chapters 3 and 4 are instances of how something that happened in the classroom assumed a quality of depth because it interacted with students' personal needs. For Michael the reading out of his piece of work by me was not just a matter of correcting mistakes but one of the esteem in which he was held by the group and of whether that was threatened. The 'real telephone numbers' made a difference to the students saying them because they were their own numbers. Often, depth simply happened by a stroke of luck. Did I have to rely on such strokes of luck? Or could depth be planned?

---

8 The notion 'here and now' goes back to Gestalt psychology, an important movement within humanistic psychology. Several ideas of Gestalt psychology have been used in education. Quite a few humanistic exercises (eg those suggested by Moskowitz 1978) draw on principles from Gestalt therapy. Legutke and Thomas (1991) have discussed their use in school teaching.

2 From the communicative approach to humanistic exercises

It was argued in Chapter 3 that learning presupposes autonomy. So, of course, does depth. If learners are given freedom they will come up with what is relevant to them. Language learning will gain in depth, ie it will take on more personal significance and therefore – it is hoped – lead to better acquisition of the language, if learners can make certain decisions themselves. Stevick (1976 pp116–19) gives a list of such decisions. They are:

- if learners want to speak at all;
- when they want to speak;
- who they want to speak to;
- what they say;
- how they fill gaps with personal meaning.

For the learner depth is bound up with being able to choose what to say. This choice can be made in a space that is left wide open or one that is narrowly defined. If left wide open, students may not be able to fill it at all. Often, for example, a very 'open' question like 'How did you like this story?' 'Would you like to comment?' gets no answer. This might happen either because members of the group do not know each other well enough or because they know each other too well. On the other hand, if a question leaves too little space ('What does the hero think in this first paragraph?'), students might feel constrained and might find the question not worthwhile. It will therefore be of crucial importance to provide the right kind of space and the right amount of space.

In language exercises this space has traditionally been narrowly defined. Students are, for instance, required to supply the right form of a word. In various guises such structural gaps have become the daily bread of language teaching. For students they provide a clear structure. For teachers they are almost like a machine that runs itself. By being mechanical such exercises can give security. They can also be boring, because there is an obvious danger with structural gap exercises that meaning never comes into play. This may even happen when exercises have been carefully contextualized. Hosenfeld (1976) has shown in an intriguing introspective study with a school learner how this student – successfully! – tackled fill-in exercises by exclusively paying attention to the mechanics of the exercise (ie if a certain cue X appears, the form Y has to be taken) and in so doing completely ignored aspects of meaning that had originally been intended by the exercise.

It was communicative language teaching (with situational teaching as a predecessor) that tried to go beyond mechanical practice and make language exercises more meaningful. Meaning was taken to be both factual information and social meaning (ie hidden intentions behind an utterance, conventions of politeness, etc, cf Littlewood 1981). The gaps in communicative exercises are therefore left for meaning. There is a large variety of them:

- incomplete dialogues in which one 'part' is left out;
- cued dialogues, in which speeches have to be made up according to cue words;
- open-ended dialogues, in which learners may decide between different outcomes;
- restoration exercises, in which sentences have to be reconstructed by fitting together two halves that have been scrambled;

- filling in empty speech bubbles in comic strips;
- filling in charts with information provided on tape;
- putting together a story from the information given in a picture strip.

Typologies for exercises of this kind like Candlin *et al.* (1981) have long been a useful tool for both teachers and materials writers. Information gaps can not only be created in teaching materials. They can also be created through the classroom situation, eg by handing out different kinds and amounts of information to participants and asking them to co-operate and fill in each other's information gaps. Defining gaps as information gaps and no longer just as structural ones has helped to shift the focus of language lessons to more meaning-oriented activities in which information is exchanged between participants. This has been a great step forward and one of the foundations on which humanistic exercises rest (see below).

There are, however, a number of problems connected with exercises using information gaps. First, inherent in the attempt to make communicative exercises more interesting than structural ones is the danger that the actual mechanics of the exercises become too complicated. This applies particularly to exercises which try to do too many things at one time, eg practise a tense form, demonstrate the use of the form together with new vocabulary, and embed all this in interaction. Tasks combining a structural gap with an information gap are widely used in today's materials. Very often their grammatical content – quite complex in its own right – never gets practised because the mechanics of the exercise, which might involve changes of speaker (ie first person to second person), making inferences about meaning, interpreting flow-charts and other graphics, etc, are not understood by the students.

One communicative exercise in a book I was using with a lower intermediate class was intended to introduce the structure *If you do the cooking, I'll do the dishes*. As a next step: *If you did ..., I would ...* was to be introduced. The exercise ran into difficulties, because, first of all, it assumed that students would get the verb forms right. This included *do*-paraphrases as well as the substitution of modals, ie sentences like *If I had to do the dishes, I wouldn't be able to go for a walk.* On top of this, in order to make the task interesting, these operations were embedded in a dialogue, which, after a few lines, required students to work from cue words connected by arrows. The task of processing the information contained in these cues turned out to be as difficult for students as putting the verbs into the correct form, which had not been practised in the first place. It is, incidentally, a frequent complaint that exercises of the information gap type leave teachers with a lot of unravelling to do. It seems as if a lot of research into structural grading, ie into how the sequencing of language items can affect learning difficulties, has passed unnoticed. Comprehensive studies like Achtenhagen and Wienold (1975) have shown such effects. Introducing a new tense, for instance, can suddenly multiply the learning load for students, because they have to learn to apply the rules of tense formation to a whole host of other forms that have already been introduced and that also have to be put into the new tense. 'Avalanche effects' like this are, in a vital way, connected with difficulty and hence with learners' needs for security. If these effects are ignored, exercises of this type fail students who might have been much better off with something less 'deep' but more manageable (like structural gaps). There is a delicate balance between being challenging and avoiding tasks the mechanics of which are more complicated than what they are supposed to teach.

Secondly, despite their claim to being authentic, communicative exercises may initially seem quite irrelevant (ie lacking in depth) to students, because they transport them into fictitious situations in the foreign country, often purporting to be 'real' dialogues between young people in the target language (which, of course, they are not). The classroom research cited above (Wesemann 1984) reported that communicative exercises can quickly become a farce in lessons already fraught with discipline problems. The very fact that such exercises hinge on class participation makes them more vulnerable to disruption than a conventional, teacher-controlled lesson.

Thirdly, it is probably not unfair to say that communicative exercises as suggested in typologies like Candlin *et al.* (1981) do focus heavily on factual information. This emphasis is echoed in the suggestions for teaching and assessing spoken language that come from an applied linguistics background. Brown and Yule (1983 p111) base their suggestions for tasks on 'information gaps', because these will show if those performing the tasks communicate effectively. These are no doubt effective elicitation procedures. They should, however, be treated with caution when used in teaching. Here they may well be perceived as stimulating tasks by some students. At the same time, because they impose roles and restrictions on learners, like deliberately taking away information for the purpose of the exercise, they may be perceived as irrelevant by others.

Factual information is, as we have seen, one aspect of meaning. However, there is more to meaning than factual information. This has been seen within the communicative framework itself. Littlewood (1981) makes a distinction between 'functional communication activities' and 'social interaction activities'. The first type is mainly about information, the second about the expression of speech intentions and attitudes. Social interaction activities subdivide into roleplay and the classroom itself as a social context. Littlewood comes very close to humanistic principles when he describes how the classroom situation can be used in communicative language teaching and even more so when he discusses psychological factors in the classroom. His conclusion shows that the copyright in being humanistic is not an exclusive one:

> The emphasis on communicative interaction provides more opportunities for co-operative relationships to emerge, both among learners and between teacher and learners ... In short, communicative teaching methods leave the learner scope to contribute his own personality to the learning process. They also provide the teacher with scope to step out of his didactic role in order to be a 'human among humans'. (Littlewood 1981 pp93–4)

Humanistic exercises such as the ones described in the diary entries are not a radical departure from communicative language teaching. They rather reinforce a trend that can already be found within communicative methodology. Many of them are indeed modelled on the information gap principle. Restricted co-operation is the principle behind 'Hotel receptionist', where it is stipulated that a guest be tongue-tied and can only make himself understood by gestures. A discrepancy in information is created in Morgan and Rinvolucri's (1983 pp48–9)

'Parallel stories', where one half of the class is told the classic version of *Bluebeard* while the other half reads a newspaper article giving the same story in a modern guise. However, whereas in exercises from a communicative background factual information is usually given and has to be processed by learners, humanistic exercises go beyond factual information. The impulses they start out from are different and the gaps they use are not so much left for factual information but rather for personal meaning. The episode *Work experience* is an obvious example. Others, that were not mentioned in the entries, are:

Morgan and Rinvolucri (1983 p63) use a story in the language lab. At various points of the story the tape is stopped. The story might, for instance, go like this: *The man went into the garden and fell into a dream.* At this point the students are asked to describe what they think the man dreamt. In another type of exercise suggested in Frank and Rinvolucri's (1983) *Grammar in Action,* students extract personal meaning from grammatical forms while practising them. For instance, the second conditional is taken as an occasion for students to relate 'narrow misses' of the type *If it had not been for ... I would have ...* In this way the potential personal significance of a structure to learners is explored.

3 Student needs

Humanistic exercises leave gaps to be filled with personal meaning. It is their aim to provide an environment for depth. How successful are they? Do students follow their invitation? It is the aim of this section to look at humanistic exercises and find out in what way they interact with students' personal needs. This, of course, is best found out from the students themselves. The following analysis therefore bases itself on written comments I had asked my students to make about the exercises in order to get some idea of how they had been received. These comments were handed in anonymously. Since they were important reading to me I kept them and ended up with about 80 of them from five different courses. This section is a summary. I have tried to categorize the comments according to the particular need expressed in them. I have subdivided students' personal needs into three main groups:

1 needs relating to the 'here and now' of the classroom;
2 needs relating to a future reality outside the classroom;
3 'realism and fluency'.

1 Needs relating to the 'here and now' of the classroom

Needs analysis was for a long time at the core of communicative language teaching. What it means is that the course designer tries to find out what kind of situation the learners are likely to have to cope with when they have finished the course (ie future communicative situations) and to determine from this what kind of language they are likely to need. Elaborate schemes for doing this exist (eg Wilkins 1976, Munby 1978). However, for students the needs that arise while they are together with the teacher and with each other are just as important as a future communicative situation. Communicative language teaching has been criticized for, as Clark (1987) put it, failing to distinguish clearly enough between 'objective' needs dictated by society, ie the tasks learners are ultimately to be enabled to cope with ('*Bedarf*') and subjective needs ('*Bedürfnisse*'). Legutke and Thomas (1991) talk of 'deferred gratification' and criticize the fact that the reality of language teaching at schools 'is still overpowered by and predominantly oriented towards future achievements ...' (Legutke and Thomas 1991 p7).

The humanistic exercises I used changed this situation, because they made something happen 'here and now' in the classroom. The most obvious examples of this were quasi 'theatrical' events involving an element of performance, like 'Hotel receptionist', where a student was offered the chance of winning the group's esteem by taking the stage and showing a new side of himself through his gift for mime. Being appreciated in this way meant investing something first. The exercises gave students various opportunities to invest what was important to them and in doing so led to more depth, ie more personal significance, be it through photos they brought, personal objects, their phone number, their birthday or their favourite animal. At their best the exercises probably addressed students' needs in the same way as my Chinese teacher had addressed mine.

The students I taught expressed several needs 'here and now':

- the need for a good climate in the classroom;
- the need for autonomy in what they were saying and doing;
- the need for security.

THE NEED FOR A GOOD CLIMATE: 'The second teacher made the lessons very boring'

There are 'soft' subjects and there are 'hard' subjects. The students thought languages belonged to the hard ones. Language lessons are all work and no play. In their descriptions of 'normal' lessons – including the ones I taught – virtually all the criticism of language classes mentioned in Chapter 1 comes up. (Student statements are – apart from some translations from German – reproduced in their original uncorrected version.)

'*I think it is good because two hours normal day English lessons would absolutely bring me to hell.*'

'*I think it's very good to do these exercises Friday second hour because two hours normal lessons are very hard.*'

'*Less useful would be normal English lessons, because then I would switch off my brain (too much informations).*'

'*... because these exercises are different from the stupid hours in the last years, in that I had to do these awful texts.*'

For the students, normal language lessons frequently meant a mixture of strain (being forced to concentrate and to speak in front of a group), difficulty (texts were the sole focus of attention and at the same time too difficult) and consequently boredom and inertia.

Humanistic exercises like those suggested went down well with a great number of students for the simple reason that they were perceived as the opposite of normal lessons. They broke up the monotony of what we had been doing. They were not about texts, they were easy and they kept the teacher at a distance. This was welcome because it removed the strain of being observed and because it opened up the opportunity of legitimately talking to other members of the class. Many students saw the main benefit of humanistic exercises as a social one: the chance to 'get to know the other people in the class'.

'The ... exercises don't change anything, they only help to (get) to know the other people in the class better, when talking about hobbies and such personal things.'

'You have more contact, then (than) only sitting in class ...'

'I learned some facts about other people in the class ...'

'The most important thing I learnt, I think, was to talk to other people in a better way than before.'

In particular, advanced groups that were made up of students from different classes welcomed such an opportunity. One student wrote that sitting in a circle had shown her faces she had never seen when they were sitting in rows.

'There was one exercise, in which a boy, I think it was Marc, had to play a sentence. I shall never forget Marc and his pantomime.' (see the episode *Hotel receptionist* on p64)

Humanistic exercises addressed students' social needs. For some students this also included social relations between the class and the teacher. Students frequently told the story of their 'Career in English'[9] as if they had passed through the successive reigns or regimes of different teachers. 'When we had X, we did ...'. Whether the subject was fun or not for them had crucially depended on the person who stood in front of the class:

'I always liked English as a language. It was important for me to understand this important language. But I've always had teachers who made boring lessons so that there was no fun in learning English.'

Students therefore wanted a good working relationship with their teacher, and one without confrontation. The relaxed 'humanistic' lessons were often seen as a step towards a 'better atmosphere between teacher and pupils'. For the younger groups, however, the theme of teacher authority – and especially that of defying it – often dominated the classroom. Problems of credibility and consistency arose with one group of 17-year-olds, because on the one hand I had set the stage for more freedom in the classroom by moving tables and stepping aside for part of the lesson, on the other there were many instances when I felt I had to assert my authority, for example by insisting on absolute silence when I or a pupil was saying something to the class. Students saw this behaviour as contradictory:

'The atmosphere was very relaxed but sometimes the teacher was authoritarian. I want to criticise this because it disturbed the good lessons.'

One message I got out of statements like this was that humanistic exercises mean different things to different age groups. The dynamics they set in motion differ considerably. Giving up part of my authority seemed for one group the natural thing to do. For another one it opened up the whole topic of independence and resistance to adult interference and everything I did was perceived in these terms.

---

9 See the episode in Chapter 5.

THE NEED FOR AUTONOMY: 'Sometimes you want it and sometimes you don't'

Has an exercise, an activity, or a lesson acknowledged students as independent individuals? Has it given them room to find their own ideas and to express them? Have students been able to make use of their freedom? With the teacher standing aside for a substantial part of the lesson humanistic exercises give students more autonomy than teacher-centred classes. Many students therefore see the exercises as an opportunity to be themselves and to speak for themselves:

'You could create your own thoughts.'

'You speak about yourself, about your experiences and not only about a text that bores you.'

'I also liked making your own texts. I liked to write my own opinion about school (you could make your own opinion).'

[I liked] 'that everybody get his own newspaper article to work on it.'

'You speak about yourself, about your experiences in this exercise and not only about a texte that perhaps bores you or doesn't interest you.'

[it is now easier for me] 'to express things I want to say into English.'

[Did you find the exercises useful?] 'In biggest points yes, because you have to think (if you do the exercises seriously) and you can speak English how you want to speak it.'

The students' wish to speak for themselves and to be taken seriously explains why some exercises that included a strong element of playing games were not received too well. Roleplays were often rejected for the same reason. The adolescents simply were not interested in taking someone else's part. They were interested in putting forward their own point of view. The only occasion when acting out a role became more acceptable was when proper acting took place, ie when a literary text was acted out and the role of a dramatis persona was taken on. I deliberately avoided the term 'games', because I wanted to convince myself and the students that these were learning activities and therefore had to be taken seriously. Despite this I frequently read comments like:

'I liked the Kindergarten games we played sometimes.'

The question that had not occurred to me at the time was whether the students felt taken seriously by the exercises. Many apparently did not. This points to one potential problem with using humanistic methods with students aged 16–19. Game-like activities may be an amusing and perhaps sometimes much needed 'retrogression' for adult learners. At the same time they can be seen as an insult by learners who have just arrived at the other end of adolescence. '*I want real problems about which we can talk.*' It was indeed this wish that gradually made me move towards 'straight' discussions at the expense of some humanistic activities, because for students the memorable lessons had been the ones when there had been a 'good discussion' (see the episode *Education otherwise*). The evaluation sessions, incidentally, counted as such occasions.

Autonomy not only means being allowed to do something. It also means using your will power to make it happen. Autonomy is action. Every single student utterance, be it in class or be it on paper, its meaning, its depth, its relevance and therefore the chances of a language item being remembered depend on the student's preparedness and willingness to say something. This fact gets easily obscured in an environment where the teacher is there to make sure that something is said and that the target language is spoken. Both the question of what is said and of whether the foreign language is used at all as a means of expression are thrown wide open once the teacher starts relinquishing control. Groupwork and pairwork have always been looked at with a degree of suspicion by the teachers who trained me. 'Once you leave them to it they will not speak the language.' This was borne out by experience:

'Every exercise you should speak to your neighbour, we mostly speak first German and translate then.'

It is indeed very tempting for students to speak the first language, because everybody understands it. Speaking it requires less effort and there is no alienation from the rest of the group. The teacher's authority may well be needed to bring about the strenuous switch into the foreign language. However, once this authority is removed, speaking English becomes a genuine effort of will.

Free will, of course, has its problems. As one student wrote:

'I'm don't interested in school.
So it is mir egal[10] what we are making.
When I leave school at 1.00h clock I'm happy.
The only interests I have are my grades.
I don't want to change anything.'

After this radical refusal to get involved in anything except the bare minimum of what the institution required, he went on:

'I know that this is an ignorant attitude but that's my problem.'

What he says amounts to a rather paradoxical statement: 'I know what I do is wrong, but I cannot help it.' The student was not the only one to describe himself in such terms. The more familiar version of students' inability to do what they think is good for them runs like this: 'I am lazy, I need the pressure', or, in their own words:

'I think we should write more word tests and homework, because there are always lazy pupils like me, who didn't learn anything if it isn't absolutely necessary.'

'I need practice in speaking and more words (too lazy to learn them for myself without any pressure).'

Mario (see the entry *If I hadn't made him speak*) had taken part in an advanced course I had taught. He was rather critical of humanistic activities. After the exam he told me that the one good thing I had done to him was to have put questions to him personally in class, to have put him on the spot so that he simply had to say something. In other classes he was left alone. It should be added that during the year the climate in the class had developed in such a way that he could probably rely on his contributions, including his mistakes, not meeting with any hostile reaction. Still, apparently, it was the pressure that had done it for him and it was this that he appreciated rather than the freedom. 'Pressure' for him meant not

---

10 German for 'I don't care'.

being left to himself. In the same way Mario appreciated pressure from the teacher to make him speak, some students saw humanistic exercises as a gentle way of being forced to say something:

'At the beginning I didn't like these exercises very much because I wasn't used to such a thing. But today I find it good sometimes to do something extraordinaire. Also if it is sometimes depressed to be forced to think about something in which you are really not interesting in the moment. In a normal lesson you sit only there and do nothing, if you don't want to. But on the other side it's really good to be forced to do s.th.'

THE NEED FOR SECURITY: 'If I had my way we don't do this'

School, lest we forget, can be a threat. It can threaten basic needs for security. Krohn (1983) summarizes research findings on students' fear of English as a school subject. Student fear may be caused by the following factors in the classroom:

- evaluations and tests;
- unfamiliar or ambiguous situations;
- lessons without a structure;
- classes taught entirely in the target language;
- tasks that cannot be prepared[11] (cf Krohn 1983 p173).

Fear of failure is one threat to the students' need for security. Fear of ridicule is another. When learning a language both are tied up with difficulty, whether it is speaking speed, infinitive constructions or an unknown word in a reading passage. Difficulty poses a threat, because it impedes performance whether in front of the peer group or in front of a translation paper. Weaker students in particular want to be on the safe side:

'My vocabulary and grammar are not very good (see my semester grade of two credits). And the semester grade is made mostly after writing-exercises, that why would it be good to make this things more often.'

As shown in Maslow's (1987 [1954]) hierarchy, security is very much at the root of things for this student. Afraid of failing the course, he is more interested in getting a pass than in sharing personal experience with his neighbour, quite apart from the fact that such sharing may be a substantial threat in itself. The latter point has, of course, been a long-standing criticism against humanism. It is one thing to talk to your counsellor, it is quite another to reveal your personal experiences to the person who decides on your English grade or to those with whom you compete for better grades. Legutke (1988) and Legutke and Thomas (1991) rightly draw our attention to the fact that disclosure of personal experience can only make sense if it is voluntary, ie if the context in which it takes place is one of respect for the student's autonomy. Humanistic exercises – like any other activity in a language class – run the risk of being subverted by the constraints of the school situation and thus become an intrusion into students' privacy. Using a statement made by Moskowitz (1978), Legutke (1988) demonstrates how the dangers of being coercive with regard to learners' feelings may be hidden in a little 'must'. Moskowitz (1978) writes:

---

11 This factor will play a role when we look at humanizing exams in Chapter 6.

The many personal benefits that can result from using affective exercises are possible only if sharing takes place. This means that students must [*sic!*] share themselves: their feelings, experiences, interests, memories, daydreams, fantasies. (Moskowitz 1978 p27 quoted in Legutke 1988 p95)

Perceived breaches of privacy were not an ongoing theme for courses in which I was working with humanistic exercises. However, they did occur, and, when they did, reactions were emotional and strong. When we did a session about religious faith (see the episode *Breathtaking lesson* in Chapter 5) one student, who was very committed to English as a subject and very keen not to miss classes, refused to attend. With another group conflicts over the assessment of oral performance and speaking about personal topics arose. When I asked one group that, on the whole, was very enthusiastic about humanistic exercises to give me a rating of how much they had liked individual exercises, those activities with a personal angle to them ('What is it like to be a first-born?') received low ratings. Disapproval was rarely explicit. It showed itself in outbursts like the following:

'I didn't like the sitting in a circle and this "stupid" (sorry!) questions. That was boring, without a sense.'

The 'stupid' questions had been concerned with personal experience. A more frequent indication that an exercise was trespassing upon private territory which students rather wanted to protect was a covert refusal to get involved. Questions were answered, but contributions were so much on the safe side that the point of the exercise – ie saying something relevant – was lost. In one exercise ('Last year's feelings') that involved telling the group things that had happened to the speaker in the course of the last twelve months, half the group opted for saying 'I enjoyed skiing', which was, as I had asked for, a true statement, but it did not do much to bring the class to life. Another mechanism that was used for self-protection was seeing the funny and bizarre side of an exercise. For example, in the autobiographic writing task which asked students to picture themselves in five years' time, a number of them chose very unrealistic scenarios. This led to a situation in which the 'investment' and 'depth' of statements differed widely. There were the ones who tried to say something about themselves and there were others who got applause for good punchlines. The effect of this, however, was, by and large, not detrimental, as the bizarre contributions were often well written and enjoyed by the group.

In conclusion: Legutke and Thomas (1991) certainly have a point when they argue that humanistic 'techniques' (cf the title of Moskowitz's book) may meet with resistance in schools:

We would say that proponents of humanistic approaches ... tend to overlook ... the possibility of learner resistance to such activities ... We should not understand this as resistance to learning, rather, it needs to be seen as fulfilling a justified and necessary protective function against intrusions by the teacher and fellow learners into intimate and private domains. (Legutke and Thomas 1991 pp58–9)

Although their criticism did not apply as radically to classes in which I used humanistic exercises it has to be taken seriously, all the more so since activities 'inviting' self-disclosure still abound in today's resource books. In a school setting these activities should be used with caution and it should always be borne in mind how basic security needs are. Open-ended activities that call for creativity and self-expression may be perceived as a stimulating challenge by some students, but as threatening by others. If someone does not like acting on stage or playing games, being obliged to do so is far from fulfilling. So both aspects of openness and risk in lessons should be taken into account. Buber (1955 [1937]) speaks of our quest for a world that is safe, calculable and predictable and, at the same time, of our quest for a world that is unique and full of risks. The organization of the classroom has to reflect both.

2 Present and future reality: 'Once I'm in Britain ...'

School, no doubt, is the reality here and now: the people in the classroom, the dog-eared book, the voice from the cassette recorder, the tree in front of the window, in short, the present. One rationale of humanistic exercises is to work on present needs rather than on future ones. On the other hand, students are not yet adults. A fulfilled present may be something desirable to strive for in the classroom, but there is no denying that students' aims also lie in the future. The classroom therefore cannot only be a humanistic sanctuary from outside reality. It must also be a preparation for this reality. School-leaving exams are one of the demands outside reality makes. Students, no doubt, are preoccupied with such demands:

'If I get the Abitur[12] stuff, its all right.'

'I think that we don't do much thing we might need in the Abitur.'

'I think translation is a big point in the Abi, but we didn't do that for one time.'

On the other hand, exam requirements do not keep students from asking how much use it will all be in life after school. In the evaluations school regularly came in for criticism with regard to the practical relevance of what was taught. The content of the syllabus was often seen as too academic and therefore not relevant enough to life. Language teaching, with its *'stupid teaching of the rules and grammar without any relation to reality'*, was not exempt from this. For the students I taught, 'depth' meant more than a good climate, security and autonomy. It included a more distant reality which they wanted to find out about, compare themselves to and ultimately master:

'Once I am in Britain I will no longer be able to read off the answer to questions from a book, but I will have to be able to think of something myself and say it.'

'Distant' can mean distant in time: ie future life. It can mean distant in space: life in Britain, America and the English-speaking world. And it can mean distant in kind: different people, different ideas, a different language. Reflecting on their own situation at school was, no doubt, of interest to students. Getting an outside perspective on this situation seemed equally important:

'The second topic "school" I like because you can compare other types of school systems, also in other countries, and you can look at advantages and disadvantages at your "own" school.'

---

12 German school-leaving exam qualifying for entry into university.

It was outside reality that the students wanted to test themselves against in order to find out whether what they knew would stand up to this test. One student, for example, was not sure whether he would be understood by native speakers:

'To learn something about speaking English in a right way is good and I like it, because in the last two years I had developed an own, I don't know inhowfar right slang and accent. I need to learn how to speak rightly with English speaking guys.'

Another student was simply interested in whether she would be able to cope with real newspapers:

'I think it would be nice, if we read an English paper or magazine (it would not have to be The Times*) so we could see how good our English actually is. I would be interested, whether I was able to eat my breakfast in Britain and read a normal paper with it or whether the food would get stuck in my throat.'* (my translation)

3 Realism and fluency: 'It was good that we spoke the language and not only to make grammar'

The foreign language is both part of the instant reality of the classroom and the distant reality of the foreign culture. Accordingly, students see it as knowledge that is the ticket to passing an exam or as a skill to be used in real life. Students interested in real life saw humanistic exercises as relevant, because they were an opportunity to practise fluency. 'Fluency' has become a prominent term in the discussion of language-teaching methodology (cf Brumfit 1984). It was interesting to see that students had their own very clear notion of what fluency meant. It seemed as if humanistic exercises were not just an opportunity to practise fluency, but as if they had, in many cases, for the first time given students a notion of what speaking freely and with reasonable fluency in a foreign language actually involved.

Fluency meant first and foremost making the best possible use of limited resources. It meant being realistic and facing up to the limitations of one's command of the language. There was a whole range of comments pointing in this direction:

'I've learned that it is not worse to make any mistakes when I'm speaking.'

'I've learned how to speak English without having any vocabulary.'

'With the help of the exercises I can make easier English constructions for to say s.th. in English.'

'The ability to speak to other people in English avoiding words you don't know by using alternative constructions.'

These may seem truisms to anybody with experience in foreign languages. For many of the students they were not (see the episode *If I hadn't made him speak*). In fact, for some of them they were probably the most important insights they got from the lessons.

Part Three
Routine

Chapter 5 **Relevant reading – relevant writing**

Diary

....

11th September

Career in English

Started a new advanced class. Many of them know me. This time it is rather a disadvantage, because they know me from 10a/11a. Once you've got the wrong image, it is almost impossible to shake it off. On the other hand: I ask them to write about their 'career' in English as a school subject during the last seven years. We sit in a circle and they read what they have written. I try hard – against all my teacher's instincts – simply to accept what they say. To nod when Robert says he hates English or when Tina claims she has no gift for languages and that whatever I might teach, it would be wasted on her. I try to react as if she had just told me an interesting fact about herself. They wait for me to react like a teacher. The fact that I don't changes the tone of our conversation slightly for the better.

9th November

Breathtaking lesson

A breathtaking lesson in grade 13. One of the topics we have to cover is 'Religious life in Britain and America'. There are various collections of texts ranging from factual reports about institutions to emotive reports about sects. All these aspects are interesting. Are they relevant? It occurred to me that these collections only look at the institutional, organizational and commercial aspects of religion and that the core question of faith has been left aside.

I decided to risk a discussion with my students on matters of faith. Quite a few of them are active in church groups, others are sceptics. How should I go about it? Simply starting a discussion in the classroom did not seem the right option because the issues are too personal to be talked about in front of a group, especially if disagreement is to be expected. I therefore chose to put my questions to them in writing, explaining why I thought initial written communication might be helpful, and asked them to write down how they felt about religion. Two of them flatly rejected this as a question they were not prepared to answer. The others wrote a lot. I collected their written statements. At home I took an extract – wherever possible an opinionated one – from each statement and typed a corrected version of it on a stencil. For the next lesson I prepared copies of these corrected extracts which I then redistributed together with the original handwritten statements. The students' first task was to read the handout and find the extract taken from their own statement. They were then to go back to the passage in their original and correct it. They read the handout with great interest. There was utter silence in the room as they were looking for their 'own' extract.

I began the second part of the lesson by asking the group to have another look at the statements in the handout. Each student read a passage and commented on it. Comments were made very hesitantly and so the discussion was moving very slowly, but there was enough material to keep it flowing.

Things started to get interesting when Volker, one of the more outspoken students ('I don't interested in school'), asked what the point of all this was. Before I could say anything, Dirk, who was visibly in favour of this kind of discussion, replied with a question of his own. Hadn't Volker said a few lessons ago that school didn't matter to him anyway? If that was so, why did he care now? It shouldn't bother him, should it?

Luckily we had a double period – almost the entire first period had been taken up with reading the statements – because now things started happening. Bernhard, a very reticent student, spoke out. It turned out he was active in a church group. He contradicted the more vocal students. I could see how hard this was for him, because others in the group reacted with irony to what he was saying. After it became clear how serious he was, others took his side. The irony stopped and the discussion went on for 45 minutes without any intervention on my part. If the initial long slog had not been followed by a second lesson, the discussion would never have happened.

10th January

Recitation

Spent 15 minutes in grade 8 working on a line from Dickens' A Christmas Carol: 'A squeezing, wrenching, grasping, scraping, clutching, covetous old sinner.' At first I had thought this line should be simplified because none of the words were known to the students. I then reminded myself that Dickens had in fact created the version I was using to be read to children. I therefore tackled the line head-on, giving the class a very brief translation of each of the words. Then I told them that it was the sound of the words, all the clenched consonants that showed us how tight Scrooge's grip on his money was. We started speaking the sentence together, trying to bring out the sound of these consonants. It was like a theatre rehearsal. I could go for a degree of perfection in pronunciation that would have been impossible in a normal language class.

22nd January

Holden's[1] escapism

Lesson about Holden's escapism went well, even the summary on the blackboard. I still find doing these blackboard diagrams difficult, because I never manage to keep the conversation with the class flowing while I am writing. Anyway, today

---

1 Holden is the hero of J. D. Salinger's novel *The Catcher in the Rye*.

it went well. I jot down some cue words which in the end add up to a diagram-matic representation of the plot. Then a rather good discussion develops when I ask them if they are materialists. Acting out some of the dialogues in the novel also went well.

14th March

With the spirit intact

Literature. Educating Rita. I take one sentence from the text: 'Survive with the spirit intact.' I ask whether they have ever had similar thoughts. They talk about soul-destroying summer jobs and the prospect of doing their national service.

20th April

Arthur's children

Arthur's children are going to school now. He says it has, after six years, changed his approach to teaching. Even after a few weeks he was tired of seeing them fill in blanks with single words. Everything they get has been just about completed for them. They only have to add the final touches to the nicely laid out exercises.

His other discovery: if he compares what his son knows with what Arthur gathers he ought to know according to the book, it is only a fraction thereof. Apparently very little of what the teacher says gets across to the children and if it does so it arrives in a rather distorted form. What are his conclusions? Make sure they write whole sentences. Make sure they write down everything. Check every single one of them has understood.

15th May

First language

Far too often I lapse back into the first language. I am quite aware that the message contained in this is: if it's business, it's in the first language. Theory has it that especially when classroom matters, ie matters of immediate organizational importance, are at issue such occasions should be used for practice in the second language, because then, so the theory goes, pupils are especially motivated to use the language. In practice they are simply afraid they might miss something import-ant and often they are far too tense even to understand things they usually would understand. In any case: I resolve to try to use English in the classroom more often.

3rd July

Kathrin's worried

Kathrin is a very lively participant in discussions, but she is very poor at any kind of written work. Asked about the reasons she says she sees no sense in writing things down. It seems stupid. If you can say it, why bother to write page after page. Her written work is usually very short. She makes hardly any effort to be comprehensible to a reader. Her spelling and grammar are poor. The summer vacation is moving closer and Kathrin is getting worried because after the vacation she has only about six months until the exam. Kathrin has realized that success in the exam will depend on her written work. Today she saw me, asking me if she could do anything about her written English. I said I would think of something. I suspect what she needs is not so much spelling and grammar but first of all an attitude which enables her to see the merits of written communication: being able to give shape to her thoughts. Putting this across can't be a matter of preaching but one of experience – one of writing experience.

4th July

Notebooks

Today I gave Kathrin and two other students a notebook each and asked them to keep a diary in English during the summer vacation. They could write absolutely anything they wanted. I told them that if they wanted me to I would read the diary without marking it or commenting on it in any way.

10th July

Rehearsal

Thirty-three kids on stage. Incredible heat because we have switched on the stage lights. It drains me of all my physical energy. When I am finished with the rehearsal all the teaching, preparing and writing lists is still to be done. The rehearsal does not count in terms of my work load. Still, I prefer this kind of exhaustion to the one after classes in which I am fighting against resistance.

3rd September

Good reading

Today, two of the three who had received the notebooks from me gave me back what they had written. Kathrin has written about 60 pages in English, an incredible amount for her. I started looking at it this afternoon. It makes good reading.

Analysis

Introduction

A colleague[2] once told me the following metaphor about humanistic exercises: 'Can you picture how they build new roads and motorways? First they do the bridges. Huge concrete things standing around in the middle of the landscape still disconnected and waiting to be linked up by the road. Humanistic exercises are exactly like that. They get you across the odd river. But there is no road. They do not lead anywhere.' Legutke and Thomas (1991) make the very same point:

> It is only when they are related to a theme that most of the communicative tasks, especially those derived from humanistic psychology, are really justified. Without a connection to content areas and representations of the target culture, the stimulation of self-discovery and self-disclosure in the language classroom will remain arbitrary and could further aggravate learner alienation, and thus be counterproductive to its initial intent.
> (Legutke and Thomas 1991 p50)

Humanistic exercises, according to Legutke and Thomas, have to be linked to a subject area, otherwise their use at school is not justified and they 'mobilize' emotions without it being clear what for. Student comments in the last chapter (see the section on 'reality') point in the same direction. This chapter tries to link the principles behind humanistic exercises, ie depth and students' personal needs, to two areas of language teaching: reading literature and writing essays. Section 1 tries to explore how literary texts might give substance to humanistic exercises and how, conversely, such exercises might help students to an understanding of a literary text. Section 2 examines writing as a means for the self-expression humanistic exercises try to stimulate and as a means for responding to a literary text.

1 Teaching literature

Literature has been in and out of the language classroom. Of course, 'humanistic education' in the old sense (see Introduction and also Clark 1987) put its main emphasis on literature at the expense of practical language skills. Until recently this was true of many university courses. Under the auspices of the utilitarianism advocated by situational, audio-lingual and communicative approaches to language teaching, especially with their emphasis on the mastery of oral skills, literature was out. Literature was back in again after it had been found out how deadly boring the useful could be.

When I first went into school teaching I asked a friend to remember her own school experience and tell me what she had liked in advanced classes at school. I was secretly hoping she would say 'interesting texts about current issues', because I

---

2 I learnt this from Eike Thürmann.

was planning to do a piece of discourse analysis on an expository text with a class. Nothing of the sort. She said for her it had only been literature that had made lessons bearable. Why? Because books had been something whole and not disjointed like the innumerable handouts they would get. A book, at least, was a clear task. You knew you had done it when you had read the book. In addition, literature was something you could talk about.

Yet despite its immediate appeal to many young learners, teaching literature is no easy task. There are several concerns that have constantly to be balanced against one another when teaching literature in the foreign language:

- concern for the text;
- concern for the reader;
- concern for language learning.

Concern for the text

Philology

The traditional way of approaching a text in the classroom might be called the 'philological' method. It is a simplified form of literary criticism. This approach tries to explore the world of the text, understand it from within and from its historical context and, in this way, elucidate its meaning. At its best it leads to a stimulating search, during which the meaning of the text and with it the 'distant reality' – one of the student needs described in the previous chapter – is uncovered. At its worst it leads to classes that are dragged by the teacher from one leading question to the next. Language teaching, it has been said, is a rigorous subject. It therefore does not lend itself easily to the openness required for reading literary works. Nor does the teacher-centredness of language classes help much. There are many student statements about 'normal' lessons to exactly this effect: everything was dominated by the text and the reader ignored. As one student wrote:

'My problem is, to interpretate [sic!] *texts right the way the teacher wants me to.'*

A literature class in the foreign language is not a class in literary criticism taught in the first language. Its purpose is different. For one thing it aims for the active use of the foreign language. The literary text is a 'pretext' for using it. For another, to the student the author's intentions are not only hidden behind imagery and symbolism but behind a veil of unknown words. What can be done? In the next section I want to make some suggestions as to how the problem of entering the world of the text through a veil of unknown words can be tackled.

Through the veil of words

Students' needs for security are bound up with all aspects of language classes. Comprehension is an important one. This at least was my experience when working with (at the time) novel approaches to teaching comprehension like gist listening or skimming (cf Bell *et al.* 1985 and Grellet 1981). One philosophy behind these approaches was that students need not understand every word of a text. They should be taught to select what is relevant and ignore irrelevant details in the same way native speakers are assumed to do this. One obstacle to putting this into practice is that students are, in fact, usually very keen to understand every single word of a text or a tape. They even feel threatened if they do not under-stand everything. This is probably due to fears of examinations and/or translation work in which every word does indeed count. In addition, it is all very well for me as a teacher to decide what students need in order to understand a passage. But whereas I have all the words available and can make a selection, students can be thrown completely by the one word they need and do not know (which is also a common phenomenon in exams). Comprehension therefore has a significance that goes far beyond the mechanics of comprehension exercises. How can the student need for security be met when students face the unknown words of a literary text?

It is especially at the beginning of a literary text, when its 'world' (ie its theme, characters, etc) have not yet been established that comprehension is difficult, because the clues to make inferences from are still very few and most key words, which will become familiar in the process of reading the text, have only come up once. Some of them may have been introduced in advance, but a lot of words are still unknown to students. The following procedure[3] is a way of easing the burden for students. Consider the following passage taken from the beginning of the novel *Looks and Smiles* by Barry Hines:

> No new records had been set when the major eventually arrived accompanied by the careers master, because they [the students] kept distracting each other, and all their attempts ended prematurely ...
> (Hines 1983 p7)

Before the above passage is read I write a number of synonyms (or German equivalents) on the blackboard:

in the end – they did not concentrate – too early

The English equivalents of these expressions can be found in the passage occurring in the same sequence (ie *eventually, they kept distracting each other, prematurely*). The class has to find them by reading the passage without looking up the words. After the students have done this the synonyms/equivalents on the blackboard are replaced by the original expressions. In a second step students try to reconstruct what they have read from the word list on the blackboard. In the above example there are only short intervals between words for reasons of space. Words can also be spaced at longer intervals through a longer passage. The exercise gives students a trace which they can follow when reading. As it is a search task it gives their reading an aim and directs their attention.

Procedures like the one just outlined open up other possibilities for teaching literary texts. If there is a difficult passage (for instance a descriptive one) in a novel that is otherwise readable, a translation of this passage can be spliced into the text. Schools often seem to be embarrassed about bilingual versions of readers. A look at Continental European publishers' programmes, however, shows that bilingual editions apparently enjoy some popularity.

---

3 For a more detailed account, cf Appel 1990.

Concern for the reader

Why is literature, despite, as we have just seen, its linguistic difficulty and despite its limited practical usefulness, popular with young learners? One reason is no doubt that reading literature allows for more depth than other activities in language classes. Literary texts narrate experience (the author's or the characters') and in so doing relate to the reader's experience. The world of the text may be wintry New York in the forties where the hero roams the streets. But what happens to him may reach out into the world of today's adolescent readers and connect with their experience.

There seems to me an almost natural affinity between humanistic exercises and literature. Both leave gaps for the reader/student and both are an invitation to fill these gaps with personal experience. There is an important school of literary criticism (cf Iser 1978) claiming that what literary texts do is artfully create spaces to be filled with the reader's personal meaning. It is tempting for the methodology of teaching literature to make use of this principle and to start approaching a literary text with a look at the depth it might have for students. The students' world then becomes the starting point for this approach; it is explored and mapped before the text is consulted and related to it. Starting out from personal experience will, it is hoped, open up individual doors to a text so that its content falls into place and in this way comes alive.

The following are a number of exercises I found useful for making the student's world the starting point when approaching a text:

Find the context

A very simple way of giving students the opportunity of supplying their own personal meaning in relation to a text and, at the same time, of preparing them for comprehension, is to create gaps in this text, ie to withdraw information from the students by for instance giving them access to only part of the text. The following exercise was used with Barry Hines' *Looks and Smiles*. Students, who had by then read a fair part of the work, were simply given the following two sentences:

> 'Have you got another boyfriend yet?'

> 'You know, him who we saw at the pictures that time.'

They were asked to think of a context in which the two sentences might occur and to note down a little dialogue containing each sentence. Their task was then to find the two sentences in the text and explain what they meant for the plot. This made it necessary for students to make connections over an interval of several pages or even chapters.

Acting the part

Shakespeare's plays usually present formidable comprehension difficulties for learners of English. Even when the vocabulary for a scene has been pre-taught thoroughly, following the actual plot can still be difficult. I found it useful to familiarize students with the plot of the scene before they read the text. I did so by moving the action into today's world. Students were given role cards giving them an identity comparable to one of the characters in the scene. Using the information from the cards they were then to act out their role. Afterwards they read the actual scene and compared it to what they had acted out before.

What would it be like for you?

Before reading a scene from *The Catcher in the Rye* in which the protagonist talks about his escape fantasies (leaving civilization behind and going to live a life in the woods), I asked the class to respond to the question: 'Have you ever thought of running away? What from? Where to?' Answers to the question were written anonymously, then folded, and put into the middle of a circle. Students then took one piece of paper each, opened it and read it. As a next step everybody read out the statement he/she had drawn from the pile and was free to comment on it. After this we read the text and compared it to what the group had found out.

Pictures of an island

Before reading the first chapter of W. Golding's *Lord of the Flies*, I showed students a slide of a tropical island and asked them to write down their impressions of it. The statements led on to our stereotypes of the 'exotic'; how it had, for instance, become a symbol in advertising. When we went on to read the first chapter, a stark contrast emerged between the aesthetic quality of the slide, which showed palm trees and a beach, and Golding's rather threatening description of the island. Our domesticated view of the wilderness subsequently formed a background to his tale of the wilderness within civilized man that unfolds in the novel.

Problems with a learner-centred approach to literature

There is a lot to be said for a 'personalized' approach. Student evaluations complained that the language needed for analysing a text was often beyond their reach and made it difficult if not impossible for them to take part in a discussion about the text, even if they had wanted to. An experience-based approach may at least have the advantage that the content of the lesson is less remote from students' means of expression. It can send out a signal that the text will – in the ensuing lessons – be looked at for a different purpose than vocabulary clarification and comprehension questions, and that the literary work will serve as an occasion to bring out personal meaning and experience. Today's methodology abounds in inspired suggestions as to how literature can be used in such a way. Collie and Slater (1987) and Carter and Long (1987) are two examples. However, there are a number of questions to be asked in connection with a student-centred approach to literature.

The first one is: It may be true that reading a literary text means filling gaps with personal meaning. At the same time it is uncertain whether doing exercises that consciously address themselves to such gaps have much to do with the real process of reading a literary work. Approaching a literary text from a personal angle may lead away from the text and turn it into a minor occasion for other things. At worst, no connection between the world of the text and that of the students is made and activities meant as a lead-in do not lead anywhere. Learner-centred approaches therefore run a certain risk of neglecting the integrity of the literary work. With one group I tried to set the scene for Hemingway's *Killers* with Hopper's famous painting *Nighthawks*, which portrays the atmosphere of a drugstore similar to that in Hemingway's story. The class saw the comical rather than the serious side of interpreting the painting and wrote funny stories which did nothing to point us in the direction of the text. A literary text is a work in its own right. Something is lost when students are left to find only their own world in this work.

Another risk inherent in an experience-based approach has to do with the integrity of the reader. Is it ethical to 'mobilize' emotions for a literature class? Should feelings be functionalized for teaching purposes? I doubt whether emotions should be a means to a didactic end. Nor am I sure if this is what humanistic psychologists had in mind. As far as pedagogic aims are concerned, Rogers, for one, implicitly makes a case for 'browsing and aimless exploratory reading for fun' when he suspects that school teaches pupils to find this 'undesirable' (Rogers 1990 [1964] p174). As for verbalizing emotions Maier (1984) has made a case for remaining silent at the right moment. In an essay about reading Dickens' *A Christmas Carol* with adolescents she observes that the text confronts young learners with questions of life and death. She argues that it is the task of the teacher 'to be aware of these questions and to keep quiet, because in this case only such answers are of any value, which are given to the individual – when the time is right – by the world around him or from within himself, which means, many years later, when the question has grown in the person. The task of teaching must be limited to nurturing the ability to live with such questions.' (Maier 1984 p138, my translation)

So how can we do justice both to the reader and to the text in teaching? When should we be analytical, when affective? I want to finish this section by suggesting a third approach. This approach is not meant to be a substitute for either 'philological' or 'personalized' approaches, because both are necessary. What I suggest is meant to supplement the two. My suggestion focuses on one important aspect of the integrity of the literary work: its aesthetic quality. The kind of approach I am suggesting might be called an 'artistic approach'.

Artistic approach

Form is no doubt an essential characteristic of a literary work. It has also enormous potential in language teaching. An important argument was put forward by Weinrich (1983b), whose article 'Literature in the language classroom? Yes, if done imaginatively'[4] was something of a turning point in the discussion about the role of literature in foreign language teaching in Germany. Weinrich (1983a) made the point that language practice of any sort means the repeated encounter (often repeated ad nauseam) with the same bit of language. He argues that such repetition can only be made bearable for learners if practice takes as its object a kind of language that has been exceptionally well and artfully structured. The language such a specification would apply to is precisely the language of literature. A third way of reacting to literature is therefore reacting to its aesthetic quality. Students can be creatively involved and at the same time do justice to the work of art when they use a literary text for the purpose it was

---

4 The original title is '*Literatur im Fremdsprachenunterricht – ja, aber mit Phantasie*'.

written for: reading it out, listening to it, performing it. Needless to say that it is here that opportunities for language practice, the third concern mentioned in the introduction to this chapter, are most easily found. Drama work lends itself to this. Stage productions in the foreign language are the climax of a school year. At the same time they require an enormous amount of work and time. One question is therefore how drama work can be made part of everyday teaching in such a way that both teachers and students can keep it up as a more regular activity. Here are two examples:

Chain performance

When doing Hines' novel *Looks and Smiles* with an intermediate class I came to a point at which I simply ran out of ideas about how to keep the discussion on the text going. I therefore decided to have the students do ad-hoc dramatizations of certain scenes in the novel. Such dramatizations were easy for me to prepare. They took the form of 'chain performances'. I would split a longer dialogue passage into smaller sections. The class was then subdivided into groups of twos and threes. Each group was given one small section. According to their ability it was left to students whether they simply wanted to practise reading this passage so that they could read it out well or to learn it to a point where they could actually put it 'on stage'. After twenty minutes a stage was created in the classroom. The right sequence of teams was determined. The scene was then acted out or read out in portions of two to three minutes, which meant that one character was played by several students. The 'identity' of a character was preserved through the various impersonations by keeping certain props constant. The props, incidentally, often just a cap, a cigarette lighter or a bicycle, usually made all the difference. What did she remember about last year's English lessons? I asked a student. 'Wearing a cap,' she answered. At the end of their scene each team 'froze' and the next one took over. This allowed me to have all students of the class on stage and not to have a division between those who were involved and those who were only spectators. I used the same procedure with younger classes when we did a 'chain performance' of *A Christmas Carol* for a parent audience.

Recitation

A second not very commonly used way of bringing the language of literature into its own in the language classroom is recitation. Recitation is an important feature of Steiner language education. After initial inhibitions I tried it out with both younger and older groups. With the younger ones I did a poem. With the older groups it seemed useful to complement the long analytic sessions on a Shakespeare drama with phases when students actually had the opportunity of physically experiencing Shakespeare's language, for instance when they tried to recite the beginning of *Romeo and Juliet*. Getting classes to do this took some persuasion at first, because it did seem odd to them. There were groups who would have none of it. However, a number of times I was told through back channels that although some of the 18-year-olds would not have wanted to go on record as saying so, they actually would have liked to carry on reciting a little longer.

2 Relevant writing

Another way of reacting creatively to a text is through writing. Writing has had as chequered a career in language teaching methodology as literature. Audiolingualism saw it in every sense as the last of the four skills. For communicative language teaching writing had to be authentic, which meant it was supposed to be used in the classroom in the same way as in outside life – hence the emphasis on information processing, such as note-taking or filling in forms.

Looking at school instruction, writing has continued there quite undisturbed by considerations that arose in the vanguard of methodology. It has done so for obvious reasons. For one thing, in writing tests pupils create the very documents on which they are judged and on which the teacher bases their grades. For another, school is not only about using writing skills, it is about laying the very foundations for them. School is about teaching literacy: from the motor skills required to achieve the roundness of an 'o' right through to the crafting of paragraphs. Part of foreign language teaching is teaching literacy. Success for pupils in a second language is therefore often linked in a rather problematic way to success in the first language because written skills, like spelling, count for a lot in foreign languages and if there is one orthographic minefield in the world then it is English.

The potential of writing

My own attitude towards writing changed when I started reading the student evaluations analysed in Chapter 4. For quite a few students humanistic exercises were, as we saw, little more than fun and games. They did not feel taken seriously when doing them. On the other hand interesting and serious discussions about relevant topics were much appreciated. When writing about these topics, their statements were often 'deeper' than the shorthand answers given during discussions. It was indeed the quieter and often the weaker students who displayed an amazing capacity for reflection and self-distance that would otherwise never have surfaced. Once they were writing, it was clear to see how the process caught on and how they ended up with statements that were long, personal and often complex. Steffen's essay (see Chapter 3) was one example.

How did such statements come about? I think they could have come about because the writing activity gave students both more security and more autonomy than normal classroom talk. It gave them autonomy because they could use their own or other resources – including the teacher – to formulate their statement. It made them, at least for the time being, independent of peer group opinion. It gave them privacy, time and therefore security. In view of this I see a lot of potential for writing to be used in conjunction with humanistic exercises. Many of these exercises, it has been argued, may be too personal to work in a school classroom. The same exercises, however, often make excellent writing tasks offering themselves as an opportunity for self-reflection. One example for this was the episode *Breathtaking lesson* in this chapter.

I have found that written tasks address certain problems in my literature classes. Such classes usually proceed through a text in a step-by-step fashion. Students read a passage. The passage is then discussed in class. They then read the next bit. This kind of procedure provides security for both sides. For the students it provides manageable chunks of work which are probably less daunting and also require less self-discipline than simply being given, say, four weeks to read the whole novel. For me as a teacher it is easier to check whether they are actually reading the text and understanding it. This approach, however, also creates a number of problems. The reading runs the risk of being fragmented and losing the unity of the whole work. It runs a further risk of slowing down too much. Some students are behind, others are ahead of the class. Boredom sets in easily.

'The novel *Animal Farm* itself would have been all right, but in the lessons it has really been interpreted to death,' one student said. How can this be avoided? My suggestion is: by restoring to the student at least part of a normal reader's freedom to respond to a text with memories, interpretations and associations of their own. Writing allows students to do exactly this. In responding to one text with another they are in good company, because this is what has kept literary history moving. Novels germinate out of newspaper articles or, as in *Lord of the Flies*, make ample use of an existing novel (Ballantyne 1857). There are various possibilities for students to respond to a literary text with writing. Essay writing is one.

Essay writing

Essay writing in the foreign language has several advantages. First, making a longer coherent statement about a novel or play provides students with more scope for their answers. They no longer respond to an aspect of the work that was chosen for them but to the work as a whole. It is up to them to choose among the events, characters, situations, opinions contained in the book. The range of options depends of course on what topics are set. I usually try to leave a choice between topics that involve imagination and topics that are more text-based. Examples of tasks in the 'imaginative' category are:

- stepping into the role of one of the characters of the story and giving a view of the events from that particular character's vantage point;
- moving forward in time and writing a continuation of the story, a task that suggests itself for many open-ended modern novels, but also for a drama like Shaw's *Pygmalion*, which, in fact, contains a prose continuation of the plot after the last act.

As far as students' need for security is concerned I also set 'conventional' tasks alongside the 'imagination gap' ones in order to allow students to take a more neutral stance and simply go to the text exploring – with the help of guiding questions – certain themes and aspects of it. I found it useful to have tasks from both categories, because it is self-defeating (and has probably done humanistic work some harm) to coerce someone to be creative. When students have the wish to do text-based work that is calculable, I try to respect this, particularly in the case of students with difficulties. In view of this I try to give clear instructions about the format of the work. In less advanced groups I also give guidance on how to structure the essay. Admittedly, this often has the unfortunate effect that a large number of essays follow the 'prescribed' pattern. I usually give three weeks for the essay to be handed in, insisting on a specified hand-in date. During this time I teach some of the aspects needed for answering the knowledge-type questions and try to keep other homework within limits.

The work handed in has shown, as a rule, that students have not only responded to the whole work but also with a whole work. Both the layout of their work and its contents have visibly received more attention than the daily comprehension questions I used to set before. The essays are also much longer and in many cases more solid. Some students use their word processors and sometimes give in to the temptation of producing page after page. The product of this can be dubious, but they have probably never written so much English in their entire school career. From many essays I get the impression that this actually is a student's own piece of work that he/she identifies with, an achievement more comparable to a picture done in an art lesson.

Another reason why students are prepared to invest time and effort in a piece of writing is probably the fact that writing is both a private and a public process. What has been written is there to stay. It can be read out to a group of people or the privacy of writing can multiply into many private acts of reading. Writers – no matter how private their communication may be – anticipate this. As a consequence the process of writing is more than reflecting on the here and now. It is also giving shape to experience and ultimately – one of the toughest educational encounters – facing oneself in the product.

When processing the essays I therefore try to move towards an 'editorial' or workshop atmosphere. This means I spend some lessons talking with individuals about their mistakes and ask them to write second versions. This also helps to create equal opportunities because some students are able to access more outside help than others. By and large the 'essay system', which was not really envisaged by the regulations under which I work, has been worth the additional effort required from me and the students. Students, of course, frequently complain about the work. One biographical essay ('Imagine yourself six years from now') concludes:

'The last years in school weren't a pleasure ... For example I had to spend my valuable time to write this stupid composition on my view in six years, without knowing what will happen until this time.'

By and large, however, the essay work was accepted by students. It gave them the chance of working at home without the pressures of a class test. It also gave them the chance of improving their grade. Some of them felt that in writing a longer piece they did actually get practice in writing correct English, which at the end of the day was what they needed in their exams (see Chapter 6).

To conclude: often analytic, experience-based and artistic approaches work best in a healthy equilibrium. After spending some time with creative tasks, there often seems a natural need to go back to the text and do some analytic work on it. I have found it makes a difference whether the approach to a work is prescribed by the teacher or whether students perceive a need for it.

Chapter 6 **Can exams be humane?**

Diary

2nd February

Far too primitive

Uli gets low grades because his word order is always wrong. In most cases it is a literal translation from German: 'In the afternoon went I to the cinema.'

Uli's test papers are full of such constructions. I have advised him to train himself to identify subject, verb, and object and to stick rigidly to an S-V-O word order in his next test. No matter what he wrote, he should make sure that every single sentence had the S-V-O word order. Uli has been reluctant. In his view this is far too primitive and therefore unacceptable. He would feel like a fool writing nothing but basic sentences. On top of this there would be deductions for poor style in the exam. I have shown him the distribution of credits I am supposed to use in marking exams: deductions for poor style are marginal when compared to what are considered to be basic grammatical mistakes like the ones he makes. Marking today's test I can see how Uli tried to stick to a simple word order. He came to me after I had collected the papers telling me he felt rotten about his English. He thought he had not done too well. What he has written is, indeed, a succession of very simple declarative sentences, but, by and large, they get his point across. Stylistically his paper is far from satisfactory, but the number of word order mistakes has gone down dramatically. Consequently Uli gets a much higher grade than usual.

4th April

Leave it

The impending exam is on my mind. So much so that it resurfaces in grade 6. We are doing, yet again, tenses. It occurs to me that I am teaching them the very same rule that grade 12 and grade 13 got wrong this morning. I tell the class they will need this rule in grade 12. Tobias retorts 'Can't we leave it until then?'

12th April

Examining

I learn a lot about examining by sitting in on a colleague's oral. He is known for his strictness. His candidates, however, are getting a very fair deal. He has prepared his questions thoroughly. Apart from giving the proceedings a certain sense of direction, this also gives him an advantage that may easily be overlooked. The person who actually conducts the oral exam is often handicapped in comparison to those who only sit in on the panel taking notes. After the event it is usually they who are in the best position to argue and support their deduction of marks with wrong verb forms and voiceless consonants that should have been voiced. In last year's finals I disagreed with the others on the panel, but I could not 'prove' my point because I had been too busy thinking of the next question for the candidate.

Working from a rigorously prepared list of questions allows my colleague to tick what candidates get right or wrong while they are speaking. At the same time he can keep the conversation flowing.

Students tell me that he can be very persistent when he asks a question in class. In the exam, however, he lets the student have a go at his question and if the student does not know the answer he very swiftly moves on to something else. By concentrating on what the student actually can do he makes sure no atmosphere of despair creeps in. I have seen this happen in other orals where the examiner was subjectively trying to 'help' a student to answer a question (probably to reassert the quality of his question) and in so doing focused both the examiners' and the student's attention on what the student could not do. The despair of such moments frequently spread to the next phase of the conversation and was subsequently very difficult to overcome.

15th May

Grammar questions

Lisa starts panicking whenever she sees a grammar question. Called upon to explain the difference between '-ing' forms like 'I have been swimming' and 'I like swimming', she goes to pieces. Protestations on my part that failing to answer these questions will not necessarily mean she will fail the exam do not help. I am getting worried that the one task she cannot do will completely occupy her mind and – maybe simply by taking up so much of her working time – keep her from completing the other tasks that would easily have been within her reach.

16th May

Not enough time

Today I went to collect something from Maria, a colleague. When I came in her daughter was in tears. She had just come home from school. Maria tried to find out what was wrong. Her daughter's class had had a grammar test. Had it been difficult? No, but there had not been enough time. Had the test been too long? 'No, but we did a relaxation exercise at the beginning of the test and it took up so much time that I could not do all the questions.'

20th May

Extra practice

I used part of the last few lessons to give Lisa and three other candidates extra practice in '-ing' forms. After some gruelling sessions they are now able to get some very clear-cut examples right. In these cases Lisa no longer guesses but at least goes through the systematic routine I have taught them. If a more complex case comes up she immediately switches back to guessing. The exam is in a fortnight's time; it is probably better to leave it at that.

22nd May

They wanted to know the basic facts first

One exam requirement is knowledge of British and American history. The group and I feel insecure about this area. I am not sure if we have done enough of it. The way such historical knowledge is to be taught is by using texts as sources and then extracting information from them. This is supposed to take place in a discussion conducted in English. It often makes teaching difficult, because if such lessons are to be comprehensible they end up being very factual and boring. On the other hand, if more intricate political and historical questions are under discussion, they become too difficult linguistically. The other day the group particularly requested we should go through the background studies topics again. Today I was doing a revision session in English with them. And, of course, my questions were too difficult. The rule we had agreed on for the lesson was that English should be spoken for practice throughout, but that any question was allowed at any time. (In theory this is the way it should be in every lesson. In practice it rarely is.) When the session was coming to a standstill, because nobody wanted to answer my questions, some of the weaker students said they wanted to know the basic facts first before they could answer any questions in English. The conversation changed into German. I bit the bullet and agreed to go along with this change. The session then went on in German for the rest of the double period. I ended up answering lots of general knowledge questions – many of them not very satisfactorily. At the end of the session we had covered, or at least touched on, most of the areas and questions that could conceivably be asked in the exam.

27th May

Pleased with herself

They did their exam today. The paper contained at least some of the questions I had been practising with them. I talked to Lisa afterwards. She was very pleased with herself, she said. She had immediately recognized the '-ing' forms and had got the grammar questions out of the way. She had felt much more at ease for the rest of the paper. None of the themes we had discussed in our long session on history had come up. However, Uli came and said how important that session had been for him in retrospect, because it had given him a sense of security. It was this certainty that 'whatever the question is, we have at least covered some of the answer' that had given him this.

28th May

Answered all the grammar questions confidently

Being first marker I had a quick look at Lisa's paper this afternoon. She has indeed answered all the grammar questions confidently. But she has got them all wrong. I took the trouble to work out a rough estimate of her final score. The deduction for the wrong answers will not be too heavy. On the other hand – I admit it would be hard to prove this – Lisa's confidence and peace of mind are palpable throughout the remainder of the paper. She has written fluently and she has made fewer mistakes than in her pre-tests.

Marking time

31st October

It is still early in the school year and I am already surrounded by a wall of test books waiting to be marked. I don't stand a chance against it. It is impenetrable. I write comments on essays. After the first 15 papers my comments all dissolve, as do the essays themselves, into one general blur.

19th November

English class test. Average grade: 3.1 out of 6. The worst so far.

20th November

Gave back corrected and graded test paper in grade 10 (nice group). Some tears. By and large they had expected bad results.

2nd February

I put myself under pressure to get through the remaining grade 12 papers. Took five hours.

10th April

Marking time. Was given one day off to finish marking school leaving exams. I watch the day pass.

21st July

Fight against time. Just ten test books.

19th October

Marking goes on interminably.

25th November

Short stories in grade 11. Hemingway's 'Old man at the bridge'. A lively discussion develops. At one point I start giving them 'hints' for interpretation because I want them to do an appreciation of a similar text in their next test. The atmosphere immediately changes to panic. The more hints I offer the greater the panic.

12th January

Put off marking papers again.

25th January

Now I am marking their papers. The whole process is focused on form and formalities. I hardly notice the content of what they have written. When invigilating an exam the other day I had a look at the French paper. I read it with the eyes of the examinee. It really reminded me of my own school days. Still the same old texts full of subjunctives. I suppose it must be the same in English, but teaching the subject somehow blinds you to the pupils' perspective.

24th May

Spent almost the entire day marking.

6th June

Took two and a half hours to do the final scoring of the papers of the advanced course. Will do the rest tomorrow.

21st January

Finished marking school leaving exams. Spent eight evenings staring at a huge A2 piece of paper covered with figures. A calculating error late at night threw me back a couple of hours. Average grade 9.6 out of 15.

14th February

On Wednesday I'll be getting 14 papers for second marking. Afraid of the work load, which I no longer feel up to.

24th February

Postponed marking.

29th April

Trying to catch up with marking. Hopeless.

16th July

Worn out. From entering figures into lists. It took all afternoon. My pocket calculator produces passes, good passes, narrow escapes, exceptional circumstances, special prizes. Often it is the digits after the dot, ie fractions of one credit, that make the difference. Of course, there is the person we want to do justice to. I sometimes try to remember all the faces, but the figures have a tendency to speak for themselves.

Analysis

Introduction

Exams are the point where humanistic fun ends and harsh reality begins. What is it that exams do to us? They do more than testing knowledge and proficiency. Exams are of educational importance in a number of ways. It is tempting for the teacher to hide behind them. 'Learn this because it is going to come up in the exam.' Students will conveniently forget about their autonomy and reproduce anything the teacher says in order to pass the exam. Exams may (and often do) narrow down the contents of teaching to what can be tested. They can frighten children, parents and teachers. As a teacher I worry about the right length (will my test eat into a colleague's lesson?). I myself feel tested in an exam, no matter whether it is an external or an internal one. Have I got the level of difficulty of the tasks right? If I don't I will be in for protests and complaints, and the marking will become an even more time-consuming task.

Taking the examinee's point of view – what is a humane exam? The first time I remember using the term 'humane' with regard to school was after my oral in maths in secondary school at the age of 18. I told my teacher it had been a 'humane' oral. He had given me exactly the same problems we had practised in class. For the candidate a humane exam is an easy exam.

Exams are a threat to security. How can such security be given without defeating the purpose of testing? An exam is supposed to distribute people. Hence there has to be difficulty. On the other hand if the purpose of examining is to access what pupils can do, there seems to be a case for 'humanizing' exams in the sense of looking after candidates' needs for security to some extent. In six years as a first and second marker of school examination papers I was time and again surprised by the 'unnecessary' mistakes candidates make under pressure. It is not uncommon for someone who writes a comment on a highbrow text about Britain and Europe to come up with forms like *worser* or *he wents*, a mistake that has never occurred in his/her written work before and for which he/she is duly marked down. So the least that could be said for humanizing exams is that they might give us a more realistic view of what candidates can actually do if they are given the chance.

But how can it be done? This chapter wants to show how exams can be made as humane as the rule book allows. It addresses four areas:

1 Making exams achievable
2 Realism
3 Strategies
4 Making marking more bearable

1 Making exams achievable

I was really proud of the first written test I set for an advanced class. It was a transfer task. We had gone through a text about national stereotypes. The paper I set made use of a caricature showing the archetypal German wearing a helmet, eating a sausage, etc. The task was to bring in all the knowledge and skills students were supposed to have acquired and write an interpretation of this caricature. I was pleased about the element of surprise which the visual element would introduce into my test paper. My students were not. They had expected a piece of text and had prepared themselves for it. They felt I had let them down. It was only after a fair amount of persuasion that the class settled down and saw that the visual actually had something to do with what they had prepared. The results of the test were poor. Making an exam achievable in this particular case would have meant being less fancy. Being fancy had worked in a relaxed classroom situation where no time pressure existed and where the rules allowed me to give hints and clues as to how to solve the riddle. Once the test papers were handed out, this situation no longer existed. Nor did the students see the slightest need for originality in an exam situation.

Making an exam achievable means both making sure it can be done and conveying the impression that it can be done. This impression can most easily be achieved by linking it – at least its beginning – in a rather obvious way to what has been done in class. While we should not only teach what we test, we should try only to test what we have taught. Note also that Krohn (1983), in his study on students' fear in English classes, mentions clearly structured classes with objectives that can be reached as an important factor in reducing students' fear. What can be done?

Split texts

One method for setting exams that can be prepared is splitting a text. The news-paper texts I used for background studies were usually too long to be covered in their entirety during class time. Since the original of the text was only accessible to me I reserved a portion of text at the end of an article for testing purposes. The actual test would then begin with the last paragraph of what we had done in class and continue with new material from the same article. I would not do this in every test I set, but this procedure was helpful with difficult texts. I got the impression that it conveyed an initial feeling of 'I know this.' The difficult parts of the text came later and were probably seen as less threatening in the light of the initial familiarity with the material. The other message it conveyed was that what we had done in class had an immediate pay-off in the test. This, of course, means that what is taught is determined by what will be tested. There is a certain risk that lessons could lose their spontaneity. On the other hand, such phases can be limited in time and dis-advantages are probably offset by the sense of direction and security I can give classes because I know what I want them to know by the end of a teaching unit.

With beginners and intermediate classes I routinely did a mock exam the day before we were writing the test. This pre-exam had the same format as the actual paper, using slightly different language items. When I first prepared a test in this way I worried that the real one would be too easy and therefore would not give me a wide enough distribution of marks. In the event, none of the tests I set has ever turned out to be too easy to produce a credible distribution.

External exams

Exams can be teacher-made or externally set. There may be a lot of leeway in teacher-made exams. With external exams, the hour of truth has come. In lan-guages such exams are usually a test of proficiency. They are expected to give a more realistic image of a student's command of the language than a teacher-made exam. From the candidate's point of view, they often seem all the more insurmountable. There is so much that should have been done for them early and so little that can be done for them late. Pupils in their last two years before the exam often stated that it seemed almost pointless to even start learning words for the English paper. For them it made more sense to cram historical facts or bio-chemistry, because these offered a better pay-off. It is undeniable that, beyond a certain level of proficiency in the language, the chances of any one lexical item learnt previously reappearing in the actual exam are statistically minute. The language quickly becomes an ocean of things not yet learnt and defeatism sets in.

What is the role of the teacher in the face of the common enemy? The one good thing about external exams is, of course, that they are indeed a common enemy, ie one for both teacher and students. For at least part of the final year, teacher and class have the opportunity to work together towards the exam instead of working against each other. As far as the atmosphere in the classroom is concerned, this is a good premise to start out from.

Having said this, it is the teacher who is tested along with the students in an externally set exam. At times success in external exams seemed to me to be a matter of sheer luck, ie of whether I had read the minds of the examination board correctly and prepared the right things. The first time I prepared students for their school-leaving exam, I was probably more nervous about it than the candidates themselves. The positive aspect of this was that I did indeed prepare them very thoroughly. The negative side was that they sometimes complained about my obsession with the exam, which without my noticing it seemed to have become the raison d'être of everything we did in the classroom. Especially after some of the scepticism that was voiced in connection with humanistic exercises I felt I had to justify whatever I was doing with a view to its usefulness in the exam. The class grew tired of this. They did want to be well prepared but they did not want their final two years at school to be dominated by an examination. This was even more true of the lower level advanced courses I frequently had to teach, in which one part of the class took the exam whereas the other did not. This difference in interest and motivation could partly be resolved by openly saying which activities were relevant for what. A more radical solution I prefer whenever it can be organized is making up groups in such a way that those students taking the exam are all in one group and those not taking it in another.

Living with examinations, then, was a mixture of astrology, thorough prepara-tion and not letting the exam dominate everything. It was a matter of showing students that something could be done and that it was worth making the effort. One first step in this direction was a system of continuous assessment that rewarded effort because it used tasks students could prepare. In my case these were weekly word tests and the essays that were to be written at home. Both counted towards the continuous assessment. They were appreciated by many students as a fallback and security net. A second step towards reducing some of the suffering exams inflict is, as the next section shows, an attitude of realism.

2 Realism

In the exercises described in Chapter 4 many students discovered that being realistic about what they could achieve helped them to become more fluent speakers of English. It became clear to them that fluency meant acknowledging the finiteness of their resources and trying to make best use of them. A similar sense of realism is, I believe, needed for coping with exams. One important strategy I chose when preparing them for an exam was therefore to train groups to be realistic about what they could do, by asking them to:

- face what had to be done;
- face what could be done;
- face time constraints.

Facing what has to be done

Fear arises over things that are unknown. It can be reduced by making them known. Facing the reality of exams is therefore one way of reducing fear. The reality of oral exams can, for instance, be faced in the form of mock exams, which are a well-known tool of the trade. In a preparation session for the oral exam I asked students to be co-examiners together with me on a panel. As there was usually a panel of three examiners for the oral part of our school-leaving exam, students would take turns being examined or being on the panel. A very simple bonus of this preparation was that students at least had a very accurate idea of the situation they would be in (the number of people, for instance, and the seating arrangement). As I was usually leading the conversation in the actual exam it also gave them an opportunity to adjust to my way of asking questions. In addition it gave me an opportunity to practice examining. None of this gave candidates, as might be argued, an unfair advantage. Rather, it gave them a safe platform from which they could show what they knew instead of what they didn't.

Facing what can be done

Those students who were realistic knew that expressing themselves in the foreign language almost inevitably meant setting themselves different standards from those they were used to when speaking in their first language. For many students, however, this was not clear. When they talked about their written work it sometimes emerged that they thought the level to strive for and what was requested of them was something equivalent to their writing ability in their first language. Steffen's essay, which we looked at in Chapter 3, is one example; Uli is another. For him the most effective strategy he learnt in my classes was being realistic about the level of linguistic complexity he could manage without making too many mistakes. He managed to get a good result in the final exam. Looking back on the course he said he had always been aware of the limitations of his English but unless I had pointed out to him what actually counted most in the exam he might not have dared to stay within the limits of what he could actually handle in simple language. The allocation of credits for the various parts and aspects of the exams was incidentally always indicated on the paper itself. Despite this, it was often worthwhile to make it clear to candidates how much successful performance in a given task actually counted for.

This had a particularly unburdening effect in the case of questions asking for a grammatical or stylistic comment. A typical question would ask students to explain why a certain tense/aspect form was used or to differentiate between various *-ing* forms. This was one of the 'knowledge' parts of the exams which students could prepare themselves for. Consequently, it attracted both their attention and their anxiety. As grammatical rules and transformations are highly teachable there was always a temptation to devote time to them. Students – their evaluations bear witness to this – even asked for it. Again, a look at the grammar questions in the actual exam paper revealed that they counted for comparatively little in the overall exam scores. Not enough, in any case, to justify one grammar lesson after another. What counted much more was the correct use of the language in answering essay questions. I tried to point out (not always successfully) that practising writing through such tasks as the ones suggested in Chapter 5 was actually good practice for the exam.

Facing time constraints

Another 'reality' students are up against in a written exam is time. Time limits have to be coped with. One way of training students for this is to do a mock written exam in the classroom. As it was only possible for me to do this on a few occasions – it simply took up too much time – I gave students instructions to get regular practice in writing against a time limit at home, by putting their watch on the table and seeing how much they could write within a given time.

3 Strategies

It would be misleading to claim that doing well in exams is only a matter of being able to handle the mechanics of it. Despite all the strategic considerations about potential pay-offs and how much a given task counts for, the actual learning, of course, still has to be done. Trying to learn is the daily reality of schoolchildren's lives. This is all the more true for those preparing themselves for an exam. If being humanistic must mean addressing the realities of normal business at school, it must also mean addressing questions of learning.

Although attempts to train students in learning strategies have recently met with wider interest (cf Ellis and Sinclair 1989), the classes I taught had received no such training. I got the impression that, as a rule, little language learning took place during lesson time. Student comments on how much they appreciated actually learning words during a lesson pointed in this direction. Learning was usually supposed to take place during homework. Lessons had the function of checking and, at best, giving feedback. The tacit assumption was that students would somehow get on with the job of learning themselves. One of the facts a system like this overlooks is that the nature of learning changes fundamentally during adolescence. Such changes are illustrated in many of the 'school autobiographies' students wrote. For many of them, learning between the ages of 14 and 18 was no longer something that happened easily and playfully but all of a sudden work and effort to be sustained in the face of flagging concentration and lapses of memory.

I cannot claim to have addressed such problems in any systematic way. The few attempts I made did, however, meet with noticeable student interest. One such attempt took place with an advanced group with whom I had decided to do regular work on vocabulary. I introduced a list of words at the beginning of each lesson, then did some other work during the lesson and later on asked the students to tell me the words they still remembered. Having rewritten the original list of words on the blackboard I turned to the class and asked them why they had remembered some words whereas they had forgotten others. From this we deduced a number of strategies that could be of help when learning words. Most students, for instance, remembered the first word of the list. This led to a realization that learning a list of words need not necessarily mean sticking to the sequence of the list but changing it or breaking it up into chunks so that the favourable 'first' position would become available several times.

In another lesson I would, again, introduce a list of words on the blackboard, wipe out one word and ask someone from the group to read the list filling in the gap from memory. I then wiped out a second word until the whole list had to be 'read out' from memory. Exercises like this illustrated the fact that for many learners the typographic image of a word and its position on a page can be of help in remembering it. We also paid attention to words that were only half-remembered. When students only had a vague recollection of what the word to be remembered sounded like or looked like I asked them to be as specific as their recollections allowed. We then compared the incomplete recollection to the correct item and tried to draw conclusions as to what had actually stuck in the memory. We came up with features such as number of syllables, stress and vowels. These features, of course, differed for individual learners.

Reinert (1976) shows how much learning strategies can differ from one individual to another, yet individuals think their way of learning is the only one. Students were therefore encouraged to find the method that suited them best. One factor Reinert mentioned was that remembering can be linked to physical movement (see also the section on TPR in Chapter 7, p116). For some of us learning words need not necessarily mean sitting in front of a desk. In one lesson I gave the group a list of words to learn and asked them to try and learn the list on the spot. They were free to walk up and down the classroom and the corridor. Students told me afterwards how often they had sat at their desks in the afternoon staring at words with no learning happening at all. The message contained in the exercise was to stop staring and hoping that something would happen, but to be active.

School often trains pupils to focus on what they cannot do. On the other hand it is acknowledged that confidence and frame of mind play a vital part in learning. I therefore advised students to watch out from time to time for those words they had, in the course of an afternoon, already learnt.

The episodes about the background studies topics and about Lisa show that creating a sense of security may be as important as getting the knowledge across to the candidates. Of course, placebo effects should not be overestimated. On the other hand, the importance of the examinees' peace of mind is not to be underestimated, either. Lisa was at ease because she *thought* she had got the grammar questions right. In actual fact she had not. Yet her peace of mind helped her to do the rest of the paper confidently. A good preparation for the exam gives students the feeling that 'we have covered it all'. In this way it creates security. Solutions, however, will have to be tailored to individual students or groups. A vital condition for this is being perceptive about the group and creating a climate in which any question can be asked.

4 Marking

Once the papers have been collected the students' sufferings are at an end and the teacher's time to suffer has come. I have included 17 entries about marking at the end of the diary section of this chapter. It could have been 170. When I was a student I once spent a night in a youth hostel in the same dormitory as a school class. In the morning I talked to some of the kids. They asked me what subjects I studied. When they found out I wanted to be a teacher they introduced me to their teacher, telling him I was studying English and German like he had done. He looked at me wearily and frowned: 'If it wasn't for the marking ...' I did not see his point at the time. I do now. At certain times of the year I wonder whether I should call myself 'marker' instead of 'teacher'. 'I have become a machine,' one of my colleagues said after a weekend with forty essays. The above entries are intended to reflect how central marking is to a language teacher's work. Teachers always moan about marking. So do I, because I think my marking load has an influence far beyond the piles of papers on my desk. Marking influences teaching by simply taking up so much time. The work that goes into preparing tests and marking them is often at the expense of preparation time for lessons. Any attempt to introduce new methods and new materials will have to consider the time constraints imposed on language teachers by their marking load. One reason why humanistic exercises made a difference to me and why I could actually use them was that they did not require too much preparation. Marking is here to stay. All I can do in this final section is make suggestions as to how it can be made a little more bearable. My suggestions follow, incidentally, quite directly from the advice just given to exam candidates: facing what has to be done, being realistic and being organized.

What markers face are piles of test books. Once these accumulate they can turn into a nightmare, because they become more insurmountable by the hour. Motivation even to touch them vanishes, because the light at the end of the tunnel is so far away, and with every new pile of books stacked on the floor it moves even further away. One of my top priorities is therefore to make sure that the growth rate of these piles does not get out of control. In trying to achieve this I have found the following of help:

If it is clear that a class has to write a given number of tests during a term, it is no use ignoring this fact and trying to improvise something at the last minute. When putting together the texts for a teaching unit in an advanced class, for instance, it is well worth giving some thought to what is to be tested at the end of it and how it is to be tested. As suggested in the 'split text technique' (see p105), one of the texts chosen for the unit should then be reserved for the test.

As a rule the extra thought and time invested in the preparation of a test pays off many times. If the tasks are well prepared, there will be fewer student queries and hence less tension for teacher and class during the test. Less time is needed in the marking process for borderline cases if the allocation of credits has received some thought beforehand (often modifications will be necessary during the marking process). It also pays to take the time to do the exam oneself, for instance to answer essay questions oneself, in order to detect potential problems for the students early. Difficult and ambiguous questions can then either be left out or clarified. Writing down my own answer also provides me with a list of items to expect in the student answers. This is helpful in the scoring procedure.

I have started making my own work load and the time I have available a serious consideration when designing tests. This means that whenever I put an item into the test paper I ask myself: Is this item really necessary? Does it tell me something new about the candidate? Do I need four sentences to check whether a student can handle *if*-clauses or are two enough? Can I achieve the same with a shorter test? It is remarkable how much marking time is saved by relatively small cuts in the length of a test paper. I also ask students not to close their test books when handing them in, so that I end up with a pile of open test books. This does not make any difference to students, but it saves me the quarter of an hour it would take to reopen the books at home and find the right page each time. One added bonus of this is that, unless I know the handwriting, I initially mark the work without knowing the name of the candidate. I also ask students to double-space because this speeds up both reading and marking.

If at all possible I put a few days between tests to be written in different classes, so that I have time to start marking and possibly finish one set of tests before the next one is written. Once I have collected the tests marking them becomes top priority, even at the expense of other tasks, because these will receive better attention once the marking is out of the way. Students appreciate being given back their corrected work quickly. If handing it back takes weeks on end corrections have lost much of their value as a feedback.

I try to be realistic, which means I try not to be a perfectionist. Correcting the long essays I mentioned in the last chapter is a case in point. Official regulations on marking the essay part of exam papers (usually a passage of a 200–300 words) are difficult to apply to long essays. I don't have the time to count the words nor to correct every single mistake. I therefore decided on the following way to save time when marking essays: I give an overall 'impression' mark, as I would do for an essay written in the first language. The overall grade consists of a language grade for correctness and style and a second grade for contents and risk-taking. This admittedly makes the mark given 'softer'. On the other hand it seems appropriate to do this once or twice a year because in their first language classes (a 'soft' subject) students are assessed along 'impressionistic' lines all the way through. Moving away from a rigid marking scheme in which mistakes are scored and compared to the number of words written also gives me more freedom to reward students who take risks.

It has been argued (Stein 1989) that students can only take in so many corrections at a time. This observation is particularly worth bearing in mind when we look at practising writing, for instance in the run-up to a test. Many of my colleagues say there is not enough time to give students both practice and feedback beforehand because the actual test takes up enough marking time as it is. One way of keeping my work load within limits on such occasions is by choosing a passage from each essay, indicating its beginning and its end in the margin and then only correcting this passage. I give back these partial corrections in class and ask students to work out improved versions. While they are working I use the time to talk to individual students about their mistakes.

Chapter 7 **A routine lesson**

Introduction

I have so far introduced every chapter with a number of diary episodes. These episodes were, in a way, special occasions. They often represented landmarks in my development. The title of Part Three of this book is '*Routine*'. Routine is not about special occasions that stick out like mountain peaks. Routine is about the long plains in between. This final chapter is a look at the plains. It is a look at a routine lesson, its procedures, phases and steps. I have chosen a lesson that might take place with a post-beginners or lower intermediate class using a coursebook, with an occasional glimpse of advanced classes. I use the procedures to be described here in practically every lesson. Since there are numerous descriptions of standard procedures for introducing words, practising grammar, etc, I have not included these but have limited myself to procedures which I assume are less well known. These will be presented in the context of the humanistic principles developed in previous chapters.

I have already referred to criticism that humanistic exercises risk being disconnected 'one-offs', Friday afternoon specials, games with little purpose. Chapter 5 was an attempt to show how humanistic principles can be linked to work in a subject area (literature) and a skill area (writing). This chapter attempts to show that the proof of humanism is in routine. Only if it can inspire what is done in 'normal' lessons will it have any lasting effect. So can any humanistic ideas be effective in everyday work in the classroom? To answer this question I want to look at the following ingredients of a lesson:

1 Greetings
2 Recitation
3 Total Physical Response
4 Revision
5 Work with the coursebook
6 Communicative deviations

1 Greetings

'Stand up please'

I am afraid I have to begin in an entirely unhumanistic way. But this is what I have done for years with younger classes. When I come in I ask the class to stand up. We say 'good morning'. The class sits down. I usually do not tell colleagues that I begin my lessons like this. Nor had I ever planned to ask a class to stand up. Like other routines and rituals discussed in this chapter this one was the result of a specific situation. In my first beginners' group of 11-year-olds I had wanted to show beginners the meaning of 'stand up' and 'sit down'. The children quickly turned this into a ritual at the beginning of the lessons. I kept it up with this particular group for the following two years. During this time it seemed to become something more or less unquestioned. Later on and in older classes I usually told the group at the beginning of the year that I had found this a peaceful way of starting the lesson and that we were to try it out for the next four weeks. After this they could decide if they wanted to go on with it. Some classes decided for it, others against it. The reason given by those in favour was that it did, despite its overtones of regimentation, make for a clear and mostly non-confrontational start to the lesson. After the age of fourteen asking a class to stand up no longer felt right for any group and I therefore never asked them to. Nor did it feel right in any other subject but foreign languages, presumably because nothing seemed or sounded quite as serious in that language.

'How are you today?'

I always followed up the collective beginning of the lesson with something more individual. Again this had developed out of a situation. I was teaching the same beginners' class the exchange 'How are you?' 'Fine, how are you?' In one lesson I wanted to make sure everybody had said 'Fine, how are you?' at least once and ended up having this short exchange with all 33 children, one after the other. The endless repetition of the two sentences seemed quite funny and unreal in the end. In the following lesson the children wanted to repeat the 'game'. In the next lessons I again went through the motions of greeting them all individually. Then I forgot about the procedure until one parent told me her son was really missing the 'greetings'. From then on I went back to individual greetings, although only with six or eight children each lesson. The dialogue expanded in the course of the year. It became 'deeper'. The first thing the class asked for was an expression for saying that not everything was 'fine'. We settled for 'not so well' and agreed that if someone had said this, I would then ask 'Why is that?', to which he/she could either answer with a reason or simply say 'I don't know'. I kept up the individual greetings with every beginners and lower intermediate class I taught. With one group I did so over a period of four years. The 'depth' of the initial dialogues varied, of course. In many lessons it was just a phatic exchange – as it would be in real life. Sometimes I used it to find out whether anything I should know about (like for instance a test) had happened in the lesson before. Very often it seemed as if this was the only part of the lesson in which students did not act out something from the book, but – in whatever limited way – spoke in the foreign language as themselves. Later on in their development, when they had become adolescents, some students developed a game of saying as little as possible. I usually asked the question 'What did you do yesterday?' and was habitually given the answer 'I was at home,' meaning 'You've got to try harder if you want to find out something.' A possible clash of wills was prevented by the funniness of the situation and the fact that the class had stated (for example in their evaluations) that they liked this part of the lesson. I had to remind them of this occasionally, because – needless to say – talking to children individually within a group of 25 to 30 is difficult, because the rest of the class can only be quiet for so long. The greetings were therefore only feasible if the class wanted them and could be reminded of some 'contract' to this effect.

It was brought home to me how much this procedure was a matter between the class and myself when a student teacher took over the class for some time and tried to ask the same 'personal' (as the class put it) questions without knowing the group too well. The class asked for the greetings to be dropped because they felt questioned and were only prepared to respond to someone they knew.

The 'how are you' part of the ritual can be given a strong element of authenticity and probably even a touch of the 'realness' discussed in Chapter 3. I usually try to speak the few sentences of the exchanges with the children as if I am talking to native speakers, ie I do not over-enunciate but say them very naturally and quickly. The 'authentic' language used in my exchanges with beginners was comprehensible to them because it was repeated so often. Stevick (1980) has given a description of the realness I was aiming for. A teacher can 'leave – or appear to leave – the Teacher role from time to time, and act the part of an Ordinary Person ...' This can be done 'through changes in voice, posture, and facial expression'. The teacher's 'non-verbal behaviour is the same that they might use at home in the living room, talking with guests: animated, engaged, apparently intensely interested in the other speaker(s) and in what is being said. When wearing the Ordinary Person mask, the teacher *appears* [his italics] to be speaking quite spontaneously, at normal conversational speed, and saying whatever comes into her mind. In fact, of course, she is filtering what she says through her awareness of what the students are likely to understand. If she supplies a word, she does so in a tone of voice which says, "This may be the word you're looking for ..." ' (Stevick 1980 p28)

Silences

Class 7b was particularly restless. It was very hard to calm them down. At one point, by sheer coincidence, there was absolute silence for a couple of moments. I offered them a bet, whether they would be able to stay silent like that for a whole minute. They did. From this we developed, for the rest of the year, an initial one minute's silence. Pupils would rest their heads on the table or simply close their eyes for a minute, after which I would 'wake up' the class. Only very occasionally was the silence disturbed by someone giggling. Again the class appreciated this as a time to calm down after the break. The lesson time it took up was no longer than what it would have taken me to calm them down anyway. I tried to do the same in another class. They refused. The suggestion seemed ridiculous to them, because it had not developed out of the class situation.

2 Recitation

Recitation has already been mentioned in Chapter 5. When looking at the beginning of a lesson I see an additional benefit in reciting poetry with classes. It has to do with the teacher's and students' need for security. The beginnings of lessons are – as we saw in previous chapters – notoriously prone to confrontation. They can be a threat to the teacher's security. Speaking for myself, a ritualized beginning gave me time to catch my breath before I started the actual lesson. Some classes said it did the same for them. It made for a smoother transition between break and lesson. They said it gave them time to 'switch'. Recitation is yet another means of providing security for both the class and the teacher. It is a simple procedure for the class because of its choral nature. It establishes, in the very first moments of the lesson, a rhythm of interaction between teacher and class – led by the teacher – that takes place in the foreign language. If we remember that the frame of the interaction in a lesson gets established at the beginning (see Chapter 2) this is more than a minor bonus.

3 Total Physical Response

I have made Total Physical Response (TPR) a regular feature of my beginners' class (cf Sano 1986). TPR is one of the so-called 'alternative methods'. The alternative methods are, along with humanistic exercises, a second area where principles and techniques from humanistic psychology have been applied in language teaching. Some of these methods include a philosophy of education modelled on humanistic principles. Stevick, in his discussion of humanism in language teaching (Stevick 1976, 1980 and 1990) has examined and interpreted the alternative methods in terms of principles such as autonomy and awareness. Two methods will be discussed briefly in this chapter and adaptations of them for everyday use will be shown. One is TPR the other is the 'Silent Way' (see p120).

Alternative methods have been topical for some time and for a number of reasons. One is the sheer radicalism of their suggestions. In TPR students remain silent and the teacher does all the speaking. The teacher gives orders and instructions in the foreign language which students then carry out (either individually or in small groups). Starting from *Stand up, Sit down*, instructions become, within a few lessons, as complex as *Take the two green books and put them behind Linda's chair.* This allows the class to follow two sequences as they move through the units of the book. One is the normal sequence of lexical items students are supposed to know actively. The other consists of words students only have to understand to carry out the orders. The class can therefore 'race' ahead – on a comprehension track – of what they are doing in the current unit. The rapid increase in the complexity of the language which they are able to handle produces a sense of achievement and mastery.

More importantly, TPR, as its name promises, considers that students not only learn with their heads but also with their bodies. The method is extremely popular with classes of 11-year-olds. It addresses their needs, of which physical movement is a very important one. TPR leaves space for active involvement, for example for acting out the meanings of words. It provides both challenge and security, because the many times an expression is heard in class along with the many demonstrations of what is meant by it make sure that all the instructions are understood, hence probably the popularity of this phase with weaker students (the potential of TPR for students with difficulties in languages was recognized early by Schwerdtfeger [1976]).

4 Revision

Before I move on to introduce the new material in a unit I reserve some time for revision. This gives me feedback on where students are. Because I start out from very easy questions it also shows students that the questions asked in my lesson can be answered. This is a necessary foundation when more difficult tasks follow in the next phase. I will give an illustration for two different areas of revision: grammar (morphology) and vocabulary.

Verb forms: endings first

One thing the individual greetings at the beginning of the lesson revealed to me was the incredible gulf between the language the book assumed the students knew and what they could actually say when they had to use the language freely. A year after the book had introduced the past tense, it was only with great difficulty and with many mistakes that classes were able to say what they had done the day before. By then the book had moved on to items like the present perfect continuous or conditionals. Part of the problem can probably be put down to the distinction between 'learning' and 'acquisition' (cf, for instance Krashen 1981). The children might have 'learnt' *he went* but they had not 'acquired' it, ie they could not use it in free speech. However, the difficulties with verb forms also occurred in very well-cued exercises. This meant the forms had not even been 'learnt'. I suspect this is due to the way in which the different tense forms are presented in the book: well isolated from each other and – in good direct method tradition – distributed as discrete grammar points over many lessons. Hardly ever are they viewed together, nor are the differences between *it has been written, he has been writing, it is written* and *he has written* highlighted. Many pupils in advanced courses are still trying to come to grips with these differences.

I therefore decided to make practice of tense forms part of the daily ritual at the beginning of the lesson. I opted to do this in a very old-fashioned way, by basing this practice on a chart containing all the tense forms students had learnt so far. For instance:

	Simple form		**Progressive form**	
	Active	*Passive*	*Active*	*Passive*
Present				
Present perfect				
Past				
Past perfect				
Future I				
Future II				
Conditional I				
Conditional II				

Students copied this chart on a double page of their exercise books. Another chart, prepared by volunteers, went up as a poster on the classroom wall. The poster served as a source of reference when the class did a written task and also for our daily exercises. I would start the exercises by giving students a (regular) verb and asking them, for instance, to put it into the past. Later I gave them the German equivalent of a form and asked them to translate it. This also served to highlight and contrast the different use of tenses in the two languages. As the next step I asked the class to turn round on their chairs, ie to turn their backs on the chart. I then stood at the back of the classroom asking them the same forms again. As a final step I did a 'chain exercise', in which one student thought of a form either in German or in terms of its grammatical specification (eg past perfect passive) and then asked the whole class to find the right form. He/she then selected a classmate who gave the answer, made up another 'problem' and put it to someone else. The correctness of answers could be checked and disagreement could be resolved by turning back to the chart. This allowed me, after I had started off the activity, to leave the running of it to the students themselves.

Words: uncued recall

Checking on whether students have learnt their words (done at the blackboard in front of the class) often degenerates into a power ritual, especially when it is connected with assessment. As there is no way round the assessment part of it, I decided to set a weekly test at an agreed date and about an agreed area, in order to keep the daily revision free from assessment. Revision then took place after the three phases described above. At the beginning of the year it was me who would ask students to supply paraphrases or second language equivalents. Later it was the students who thought of words and forms to ask each other.

One alternative to giving students first language equivalents or paraphrases as cues is 'uncued recall' (suggested by Stevick 1976 p79). I have found this procedure useful because it has helped me to move towards more depth and autonomy during the revision of words. When doing 'uncued recall' students try to come up with as many words from a text/a unit/a week's work as they can remember without the help of the book. Only after they have exhausted their memory do they go back to the book and double-check. Uncued recall can be done at the beginning of a lesson to revise previously learnt vocabulary or during the lesson when a new passage has been introduced. One advantage of this procedure is that it individualizes revision. Students come up with 'their' words. They say something only they can say. From a mnemonic point of view words revised in uncued recall are said to have a better chance of being remembered. The technique can also become a co-operative effort, for instance when the whole class is asked to assemble a list of words (belonging to a particular lesson or word field) on the blackboard. Chalk is broken up and given to the class who then fill the blackboard with their words. This 'word cloud' on the blackboard often serves as a starting point for further exercises. With more advanced learners it is sometimes a good start to a course to ask them to write down ten words they have recently learnt. In my classes, there were often stories attached to such word lists which then led on to a discussion about language lessons (were these useful words?) and learning (why did students remember these words and not others?). In this way student autonomy and depth could be enhanced during an ordinary classroom activity.

Revision of words can be a smooth entry to the introduction of new lexical items. One prerequisite for students to be able to say something in the little exchanges at the beginning of the lesson is knowing enough words. I noticed this when I was teaching beginners. Autonomy and depth, ie the power to say what you want to say, means, in the first place, having the words for it. By 'words' I do not mean the capsules or skeletons provided within a communicative syllabus (ie making a polite request with *Could I* ...), but rather the meat on such skeletons: content words. With my beginners' group it quickly became necessary to proceed to such words (animals, fruit, hobbies, family, jobs ... and again animals). We delved into one word field after another. There was a great hunger for words in the class. In the end, not all of them learnt all the words. But for Dirk, being able to say that he had a ferret at home made all the difference.

With advanced classes I regularly introduced five to ten new words in each lesson. The reason for this was that these classes often said that for them vocabulary problems were one of the most threatening and insurmountable obstacles in the exam. Trying to make this aspect of the exam achievable, I wanted to demonstrate that something could be done to overcome these obstacles if we started early and worked regularly. Regularity, I hoped, could at least serve as a demonstration that some progress was possible. In order to give the introduction of new words a sense of direction I linked the vocabulary to books we were to read later in the year. Since success or failure in reading these books hinged on having sufficient vocabulary, it made sense to introduce them in good time and thus provide a smooth entry into the text. This was particularly true for the Shakespeare play that was obligatory in certain courses. It was, in fact, the very advanced classes that often appreciated such regular vocabulary work most. They often perceived their course work as a succession of disconnected handouts with very little sense of coherence in the course structure as a whole and equally little guidance as to what they were actually supposed to learn. Regular revision was appreciated against this background. 'It was one of the rare occasions when I really learnt words,' one student commented. He rated this part of the lesson much more highly than any of the humanistic exercises.

5 Work with the coursebook

Coursebooks usually contain their own methodology. The following are a few techniques that can be used with practically any course material, irrespective of how this material is structured.

Lively dialogues: Tony and Ilona

After pre-teaching the necessary words for a unit in the book one of the first tasks for the teacher is to present the text. In the case of a dialogue there is the difficulty that two (or several) speakers are needed for the different roles. This is usually solved by playing a recording of the dialogue. Recordings have the advantage of presenting more authentic language. However, as we saw in Chapter 3 there is more to authenticity than authentic recordings. True to the principle 'something of your own', I occasionally did my own dialogues. All it required was reading the dialogue in the book, checking on the new words, and two glove puppets known to the class under the names Tony and Ilona. Tony and Ilona became our companions. They were good fun for everybody because they could say all the things authors and editors of nationally used textbooks would never dare to put into a dialogue. Blackboard drawings were the backcloth to their little dramas about losing keys, about jumping into the deep end of swimming pools and being saved from drowning, and about ownership of black taxis. 'Black Taxi', incidentally, soon became a character in its own right. Originally a model of a London cab meant to introduce the word *taxi*, it quickly developed a personality of its own. The class had long and deep conversations with Black Taxi. I held it up in front and asked if there were any questions. The 11-year-olds were remarkably clever in using bits from the questions I had asked them at the beginning of the lesson along with bits from the book for drawing out the conversation with Black Taxi. When one of the kids asked Black Taxi 'Have you got children?' his question led to an ingenious two-page homework showing Black Taxi's family tree.

Pronunciation: word reading and the 'Silent Way'

One important task when working on a passage in the book together with a class is practising correct pronunciation. I use the following procedure for training students to match the visual image of the spelling of a word to its pronunciation. I am aware that there are different schools of thought as to when the graphic representation of a word should be introduced in a course. My suggestion is not meant as an intervention in this debate but rather as a tool teachers can use whenever they think the circumstances are right. The procedure is an adaptation from another 'alternative method': the 'Silent Way'.

'Silent Way' means the teacher – and not the students – remains silent throughout a lesson. The teacher provides students with visual material (eg coloured charts indicating the relationship between spelling and sounds in the foreign language). The group tries to work out the right pronunciation with the help of these materials. They use the teacher's non-verbal feedback and each other. In relying on their own resources they not only learn pronunciation but also to be autonomous and to be more aware of their own resources.

It is received wisdom to teach the pronunciation of a word (or a sentence) by giving students a model and having them imitate it. I tried to vary this procedure by using the following sequence. Before students listened to a passage I would put some words which were difficult to pronounce on the blackboard and ask students to listen out for them. At the end of the passage I asked them to read out the words on the blackboard. When working on these words I tried to stay totally silent and only give non-verbal feedback to the class, using gestures meaning 'almost there', 'I am not sure about this', 'no', 'try to remember what your neighbour just said' and 'that's it'. The class had to listen to and co-operate with each other until they got the pronunciation of the word right. Working with this kind of non-verbal feedback took some training, both for me and for the class. Telling a pupil in the last row of seats simply by eye-contact or a gesture that it was his/her turn, required both practice and a lot of concentration from myself and the class. It was, however, this atmosphere of intense concentration that I liked most when working in this way. Needless to say, this concentration could not be expected to last any longer than a couple of minutes. A more advanced version of the exercise was simply to put the words on the blackboard and ask students, without prior listening, to arrive at the pronunciation by trial and error with occasional non-verbal feedback from me. Once the correct pronunciation had been established students could volunteer to read out the whole list on the blackboard. I had expected they would find this boring. Quite the contrary. Usually up to 90 per cent of the students wanted to read out the words or expressions again. They did not think that the task was too elementary for them. This was also true for intermediate learners. Weaker students in particular appeared to get a sense of satisfaction and above all security out of this. So, for a couple of minutes, I could slightly change my role as a teacher from model to that of provider of feedback.

Playing around with meaning: bilingual techniques

After a passage has been introduced and read the language presented in it is to be practised. Coursebooks usually contain a wide range of exercises for processing the language introduced in a text. The following procedures can be used in addition to such exercises. They make controlled use of the first language for demonstrating meaning. Bilingual exercises have in the past – at least in Germany – been surrounded by some controversy because they were seen as violations of the basic tenets of the direct method. In teacher training the ability to teach a good direct method lesson is still (and probably not without justification) seen as the hallmark of a qualified teacher. Criticism of the direct method lessons has, however, come from teachers who ended up spending half the lesson explaining words when a translation might have taken only a few seconds. It has also come from those at the receiving end, ie parents and pupils who complained they did not understand the explanations. Their reservations found theoretical backing in the work of Butzkamm (1980), who made a case for bilingual methods. What I want to do in this section is give some examples that show the usefulness of bilingual procedures for creating both manageable and challenging tasks.

The first example is *retranslation*. After a passage has been read and worked through I give students the German equivalent of phrases they have read in the text. I give them in the same sequence as they occurred in the text and space them at regular intervals. Students are to find the English expressions in the text and read them out. Unlike in the exercise described in Chapter 5 (p91), this time the aim is to do a quick revision of language items that have just been introduced. Again, students in my classes did not think this task was primitive but took it very seriously. Once established, the exercise helps to create an atmosphere of concentrated listening. In a further step, retranslation can be turned into a more meaningful 'bilingual drill'. The following suggestion is made by Butzkamm (1980 p104). Students start from a Charlie Brown cartoon. One of the sentences it contains is *He'd make a good human being*. When presenting the dialogue the teacher supplies the German equivalent ('*Er würde einen guten Menschen abgeben*') together with the original sentence. The first language cue is then varied, prompting sentences like *He would make a good teacher*. Step by step the various 'slots' in the structure are replaced by other lexical items, changing the original sentence to *These boys certainly would make bad fathers*. Butzkamm's lesson transcripts show how exercises like these can be clearly structured and controlled and at the same time, half playfully, refer to the 'here and now' of the classroom, thus moving towards real communication and more depth. One of the most desirable things to happen in a language class is, of course, exactly this: an exercise intended to practise a language item assumes a quality of depth and turns into a communicative event. It is such moments I want to turn to in the final section.

6 Communicative deviations

The routines and procedures presented in the five preceding sections can give a structure and a baseline to a lesson. They could be likened to the beat in a piece of music. However, music only comes to life when the baseline is left and when the theme contained in it is developed and varied. At the beginning of Chapter 4, when we first turned to the question of language teaching method and humanistic principles, I asked the question whether depth can be planned. In what followed, methods were examined in terms of how they could be conducive to depth. Coming back to the original question now, I would answer that depth can only be planned so far. There can be recipes for routines. Whether they come to life is a matter of opportunities seized or missed. The success of such interventions and deviations from the planned course of a lesson will partly depend on the teacher's grasp of the situation and the mood of a class. At the same time they depend on the routine a teacher has. The following suggestions are therefore not meant to supplant routine work. Used skilfully within such work, they might, however, bring a tired class back to life. One merit of the humanistic exercises described in the last chapter is that a teacher, having done a number of them, may be able to take a new look at conventional material and in this way open it up to student initiative. The following is a collection of examples.

Ghosts

With one intermediate class I was reading *A Christmas Carol*. The class very much enjoyed reading and playing the ghosts. We therefore had ghosts appear in other exercises, too. We took, for instance, a piece of dialogue from the book. Two speakers would perform this dialogue. Two 'ghosts' stood behind them and said, after each sentence, what the speakers 'really' thought.

'Would you want to have lived one hundred years ago?'

In one advanced class I was doing an exercise in which students had to decide whether a definite article was needed to fill a gap in a text. One sentence read: *The desire to live and improve ... life is strongly implanted in men* (Fisch *et al.* 1977 p117). The students worked their way from one 'article or not' decision to the next. At one point I realized that at no point of the exercise did content matter in any way. Out of sheer frustration with the autopilot on which my lesson was running at that moment I asked the class to stop watching out for definite articles for a moment and answer the question for me, if they really thought that there had been any progress? They did not answer and seemed surprised at the question. I insisted and rephrased the question, telling them about an advert I had recently seen. It showed a swimming pool in the good old days, quite idyllic, and went on to give a glossary of all the diseases and health hazards bathers in the good old days would have been exposed to. I asked the class 'Would you want to have lived one hundred years ago?' We talked for the rest of the lesson. For a time, we forgot about the mechanical side of the structural gap exercise and the exercise became relevant to the students. This principle can – as Frank and Rinvolucri (1983) showed – be used almost anywhere.

Interpreting

Use of the bilingual techniques described so far is not confined to beginners' and intermediate classes. They can also be used as a challenge and an opportunity for advanced students to experience the potential of the language they have learnt from a text. One exercise providing this opportunity is bilateral interpreting. It works like this:[5] There are three parties. A specialist/politician/historic figure enacted by the teacher, an interviewer from abroad played by a student, and an interpreter played by various members of the class. The interviewer gets a list of questions prepared beforehand by the teacher in the first language. These questions are simply translations of comprehension questions already dealt with during the initial reading of the passage. As a lead-in, translating these questions into English is practised. The interviewer then asks his/her questions in the first language, and these are translated by someone into English. The teacher answers in unscripted speech initially using language from the text, building in a lot of redundancy in the form of repetitions and rephrasings and also carefully introducing English expressions which are needed for the translation of the next question addressed to him/her by the interviewer in German. Often students who could not speak English at all fluently found they could interpret into their own language rather well. They got a sense of achievement out of this. Apart from practising a skill, the interpreting practice I have just described also made a good comprehension exercise, and gave students much needed exposure to the spoken form of the language, an exposure basing itself on a written text that had already been understood. In one exercise I handed over complete control to the student acting as interviewer. In the exercise she was interviewing a Canadian exchange student. The exercise had been moving very hesitantly until it suddenly occurred to the interviewer that she could ask her Canadian partner questions of her own. She left her script and asked the questions she was really interested in. The conversation became lively, when the class saw that they had the same freedom. From now on the exchange student was answering questions that had not been prepared. Her speech became more fluent and authentic.

Conclusion

I am aware that some of the suggestions I have made, especially those made for the opening of a lesson, may appear to be rather old-fashioned and indeed could be open to misunderstanding. People's biographies are, after all, full of school days that were experienced as empty rituals. The reason why I have tried to make a case for rituals and routines is that they provide both security and stability. This view finds support in research literature. Studies of school classrooms have acknowledged the value of rituals in this respect:

> A teacher's relationship with his or her class is based on constant and continuing contact; it therefore needs stability and finds change unsettling. Stability is provided by classroom routines which support shared expectations of behaviour. (Prabhu 1987 p103)

---

5 For a more detailed account, cf Appel (1985).

Van Lier comes out even more explicitly in favour of rituals, defending them against any accusation of not being authentic:

> There may be several valid arguments for the maintenance of a ritual element in the language classroom, quite apart from any direct language-learning benefits ... Throwing out chorus work, display questions, repetition, and so on, since they are not 'authentic' communication ... may constitute premature surgery. (van Lier 1988 p227)

Admittedly, the danger that rituals and routines become devoid of sense and that they are merely imposed by authority is always present. I would therefore like to stress again that the routines and rituals suggested in this section only worked in a context where they had developed out of the classroom and were based, at least partly, on a 'contract' agreed on by the group. Nor should it pass unnoticed that the rigours of ritual were very often tempered by humour.

Conclusion **Beyond year six**

These were my first six years as a language teacher. Books, especially those that tell a story, have a beginning, a middle and an end. So does this one. In contrast, everyday life – at school and elsewhere – only seems to have a middle. There is something amorphous to it. When going through the diary entries that were to become the backbone of this book, I was not so much struck by the little dramas they contained but rather by the enormous amount of repeated experience recorded in them. I was reminded of a dialogue between two teachers in a novel by J. L. Carr:

> 'I've never been spoken to like this before in all my thirty years experience,' she wails.
> '*You* have not had thirty years experience, Mrs Grindle-Jones,' he says witheringly. '*You* have had one year's experience 30 times.'
> (Carr 1984 p128)

Experience can be something alive or something dead. It can be something that is renewed day by day or a fossil. How often has the sentence 'In my experience' been used to say 'I've seen it all, I've tried it all, forget it'? How many new ideas have been cut short in this way? Yet it was the safety of repeated experience called routine that I wanted most when I began teaching. Routine was what I had by year six. So, are routine and experience the aim of my development as a teacher – or its end?

When I started work on this book, my first six years lay just behind me. Now, at the time of writing and rewriting this conclusion, they lie a great deal further behind. Work on this book has taken almost as long as the period of time it describes. I have not accumulated Mrs Grindle-Jones's number of years yet, but I do occasionally ask myself what it must be like. Having written about development and change, I want to conclude these pages with a quick look at the problems I both witnessed and experienced after year six (Section 1) and some solutions to them (Section 2).

1 Problems beyond year six

Originally, I had taken time out from school to work on this book. I have since gone back to teaching. It was like stepping back into the scenes described on these pages and reliving some of the experiences. Some things had, of course, changed. One was my age and that of my colleagues. I have since had the opportunity to look back on what I have written from the point of view of year ten and beyond. I found some problems to be less acrimonious than in year one. Discipline was one of them. After initial difficulties it moved to the background. Which of course does not mean it is no longer there. Seasoned practitioners have owned up to this:

> After many many years on the job I still keep having the same dream: I am standing in front of a class and try to get a grip on them. The pupils run riot and laugh their heads off over how helpless I am. (Fölsch 1993 p22, my translation)

Discipline apart, what are the problems facing teachers beyond year six? I found they were the following:

1 physical strain;
2 monotony and repetitiveness of the job;
3 age gap;
4 lack of a sense of purpose and value.

I will look at each problem and possible solutions in the light of the ideas and observations put forward in this book.

1 Physical strain

To do justice to Mrs Grindle-Jones: 30 years in the classroom is a long time. It is undisputed that teaching at schools pushes many teachers to their limits and, in the course of their career, drains them of the best part of their enthusiasm. Nor has the task become easier:

> It seems a reasonable hypothesis that teaching in the public system over the past few decades has become more demanding, in the sense of being more complex, more open-ended, and placing more responsibility on the individual teacher and the immediate work group. It also seems likely that the shape of the pressures on teachers has changed, from a situation where the main pressure came from an extremely hierarchical management, to one where the main pressure comes from a much more varied and much less submissive clientele. (Connell 1985 p125)

Experienced teachers are subject to much the same pressures as beginners. They might react more appropriately. In terms of physical health, however, they may be even more at risk, because of their age and because they have too often trained themselves to ignore physical symptoms of stress. 'Burn-out' has become a fashionable term. Leuschner and Schirmer describe what it means for teachers:

> After one to two decades they have reached their limit. This happens at an age which is commonly taken to be the climax of professional performance, achievement, experience and power. (Leuschner and Schirmer 1993 p6, my translation)

2 Monotony and repetitiveness of the job

Justice for Mrs Grindle-Jones yet again. Work at school is bound to be repetitive, because it is cyclical in nature. The week's timetable repeats itself. So, deceptively, do the generations of pupils. It is Monday morning and 10.20, so it must be 6a again, as it was last week. Wesemann (1984) has argued that the time-slots distributed evenly over days and weeks lead teachers to expect that nothing new will happen within each slot, no matter how different the situation might be. As my head said: 'As a parent you experience adolescence once, as a teacher thirty times.' What was a special event in year one becomes all but boring in year six. Never mind year ten, twenty ...

Add the often negative encounters with classes, parents, colleagues and superiors, and it is no longer surprising that teachers insulate themselves from their work. After a certain measure of disappointment and frustration at school the natural reaction is one of inner emigration: blot out everything connected with school, immunize yourself against it. Needless to say this is hardly a fertile ground for new ideas.

3 Age gap

It was mentioned in Chapter 1 that isolation is one stress factor of the job. Isolation gets worse once the age gap between the students and the teacher widens. Young teachers, it is said, find it easier to relate to young people. 'The lines between them and me used to be open,' one colleague commented, 'now they are closed.' Recent studies (Schultze 1993) on German society have shown that age difference has become a factor defining social identity. In particular the generation of teachers who have based their social identity on being the younger generation and who, for this reason, once related well to students, must find themselves isolated when, today, they are confronted with a younger generation whose outlook and values are totally different. I have occasionally felt this gulf.

4 Lack of a sense of purpose and value

No longer having a line open to the 'clientele' means there is no feedback, in particular no positive feedback. I don't know about the social status of teachers in other countries, but in mine it is, according to recent surveys, low. Education has been in and out of political favour. It was once seen as a key to solving the problems of society. As the attitude towards virtually all professionals has become more critical it has also become more critical towards teachers. I have frequently had to defend myself and what I was doing not although but *because* I was a teacher. Berliner stresses the need to 'build pride in the much-maligned profession of teaching' (Berliner 1987 p81). Lack of appreciation sooner or later results in lower motivation. This in turn leads into a vicious circle. Enjoyment of teaching depends to a considerable degree on how much a teacher invests in terms of preparation and emotion. If less and less is invested in the job, the job gets less and less enjoyable, which then leads to even less investment ... What I am describing is not a theoretical problem. It is a problem for all concerned, because problems of the teacher are also problems of student motivation. Sustaining the momentum and enthusiasm of a class of adolescents is no easy task at the best of times. It is an impossible one for those who lack enthusiasm themselves. The question I want to address in the remainder of this conclusion is how this negative cycle can be broken and turned into a positive one.

2 Solutions beyond year six

I want to look at three areas where solutions to the above problems might lie:

1 teachers' career structure;
2 the role of research;
3 teaching as an art.

1 Teachers' career structure

I personally had the luck to be able to take an extended break from teaching. I returned to the job refreshed. The routine I still had from my first six years together with some new perspectives made teaching a much more enjoyable experience than it would have been otherwise. My time out of school was a private decision, financed privately. I think the question of whether teachers should be given breathing space beyond their summer holidays is worth serious consideration. There are, I believe, some educational systems which consider sabbaticals necessary not only for university teachers but also for school teachers. This may sound like asking a lot. I am aware of the practical and financial difficulties involved (although it would be worth looking in comparison at the cost of teachers' health problems, including early retirement). Apart from counteracting health problems, a sabbatical would be an opportunity for renewal. It need not be a course in teaching methodology. Whatever has an educating effect on teachers, especially any artistic, theatrical and musical activity, would stand a high chance of having an educating effect on students when this teacher returned to the classroom.

Returning from a year out would also mean returning from a world that is different from school. Teachers are expected to prepare students for the world outside school. Chapter 4 has shown the quest for reality expressed by students. Preparation for reality can only come from those who have experienced it themselves, ie from those who have, once in a while, left the world of the classroom. In one school where I was trained, there was a teacher for whom teaching was, after a career as a photographer and as a graphic designer his third profession. He was said to have singularly few difficulties with students. He was about fifty and apparently suffering from none of the usual syndromes of the profession. His example shows that a difference in age need not necessarily lead to alienation. Both the young and the experienced teacher have something to offer students. 'They want a teacher rather than a friend,' I was told before I started work. Much as I objected at the time, I have found a grain of truth in this. Teachers are of interest to students exactly because they are different, because they represent a different, new and outside experience (provided they have had this experience). Keeping the lines open and being able to communicate this experience probably requires greater effort in year ten than it does in year one. However, if the encounter between the two worlds takes place in an atmosphere governed by the attitudes described in Chapter 3, ie one of trust, respect and interest, it may well succeed.

Good relations with students are, of course, not only a matter of a good atmosphere. They are also a matter of good teaching. Good teaching is what I want to turn to in the next two sections, because it is a source of professional enjoyment and self-esteem, and might also serve to reverse the vicious circle mentioned earlier.

2 The role of research

How can teaching be improved? One obvious source of improvement would be research. In the introduction I have referred to the hierarchical and hence somewhat uneasy relationship between research and teaching. More recently a number of suggestions have been made as to how research could help in the renewal of language teaching in schools. Widdowson (1984) has made a case for the 'incentive value' of theory and research and would like to see more teachers in the role of researchers. Projects in curriculum renewal (Clark 1987) no longer see teachers as mere implementors and envisage a more active role for them (cf also Nunan 1989). Altrichter (1990) has presented an extensive study on the potential of teacher-initiated research. All these suggestions aim at making the relationship between theory and practice more dynamic than I have described in the introduction. This is certainly a step forward. However, I sometimes wonder, since it is considered desirable to have teachers in the role of researchers, if it might not be equally desirable to have researchers as teachers. Research has the unfortunate tendency (unfortunate for those at schools, I mean) to help researchers graduate out of the classroom. Both theory and practice could profit from an exchange taking place in both directions. Schools would benefit from personal and first-hand experience of new concepts and teaching ideas. Theory, and especially teacher training, would benefit from a personal experience of the situation in which innovations and teaching suggestions are supposed to work. If one year's experience 30 times is not what we want for teachers, then neither is one year's experience 30 years ago for those who train them.

My other query about the teacher-as-researcher model is that even if teachers do become involved in research, the teaching is still there to be done. Moreover, the fundamental differences between teaching and research remain. The aims, methods and priorities of research are legitimate in their own right, but they differ from those of teaching. Research is about experimentation, about proving and disproving hypotheses. Teaching has other priorities. This is not to say that it could not profit from basing itself on theoretical reflection. How the outcome of such reflection translates into practical action is, however, a more indirect and complex process than that suggested by a concept like 'application'. Theory probably influences practice via attitudes, notions and metaphors. The latter have recently attracted research interest (cf Thornbury 1991a, 1991b). A knowledge of findings in the field in second language acquisition might, for instance, change a teacher's attitude towards students' mistakes – a change badly needed at a time when school teaching is still almost exclusively concerned with taking off marks for mistakes in verb endings. Notions and metaphors generated by research such as 'fluency/ accuracy' or 'learning/acquisition' might inspire the hundreds of decisions a teacher makes in the course of a school day. If the danger of theories and metaphors becoming dogma is avoided they might provide the teacher in the classroom with a measure of critical distance from the constraints and rules imposed by the institution. Since research is an expression of interest in its object, it might also lead to more empathy, provided its 'subjects' are really seen as subjects, ie as persons. Theory and research might influence attitudes and attitudes are, as we have seen, a vital ingredient for good teaching. Good teaching, however, is more than using the right, ie the empirically proven method (if we neglect, for a moment, the question of whether such proof really exists). It needs on-the-spot reactions, a light touch, wit, humour, routine, departures from routine, principles and U-turns at the right time. Many of these do not come easily to the well-ordered world of empirical research. It is for these reasons that I finally want to turn to the notion of teaching as an art.

3 Teaching as an art

Teaching as an art is a concept belonging to bygone days. It appears in publications written decades ago (cf Highet 1965 [1951]). 'Scientific' approaches to language teaching have since been the model in the field and have, not unexpectedly, looked with suspicion at the notion of teaching as an art. Halliday *et al.* (1964) wrote: 'Linguistics is a science, teaching is an art' (Halliday *et al.* 1964 p211). This may sound like equal partnership, but a closer look reveals that the teacher's art is seen as little more than attention to minor details, because it is only for 'fine detail' (Halliday *et al.* 1964 p211) that 'the teacher's classroom experience should be followed'. Achtenhagen and Wienold (1975), in a major study of the role of materials in teaching beginners, state as one of their aims that teaching should no longer have to rely on 'tricks of the trade' and that teachers should be provided with empirically tested recommendations. There has been a certain shift of emphasis since Schön (1983) argued that what is needed for successfully coping with the uniqueness and flux of situations of professional practice is more than straight deductions from scientific disciplines:

> It is no accident that professionals often refer to an 'art' of teaching or management and use the term *artist* [his italics] to refer to practitioners unusually adept at handling situations of uncertainty, uniqueness, and conflict. (Schön 1987 p16)

In the wake of such renewed interest in practical action, teachers' experience and skill have received more attention in research:

> ... studies have sought to understand teachers on their own terms and in their own language by attempting to elicit often implicit and only partially articulated elements of teacher knowledge that guide teachers' actions in specific contexts. (Zeichner *et al.* 1987 p22)

Eisner (1979) has very explicitly put forward the notion of teaching as an art. He considers teaching to be an art in the sense that 'teachers, like painters, composers, actresses, and dancers, make judgements based largely on qualities that unfold during the course of action ...' The ends they achieve 'are often created in process' (Eisner 1979 p176). Note how this view of teaching ties in with that presented in Chapter 1. The 'qualities unfolding in the course of action' are part of what makes the teaching situation unique and incalculable. Only now uncertainty and uniqueness are no longer seen as a disturbance or a threat, but rather as the 'material' on which the art of teaching can be practised. In Chapter 2 flexibility was advocated as a skill for coping with contingencies. In Chapter 5 a case for communicative deviations was made. Teaching as an art can be seen as a refinement of these skills. They are part of Eisner's definition of art: being able to 'work on' a situation as it unfolds 'during the course of action'. It means being able to integrate the unforeseen while not losing the general structure of a lesson, or in Elbaz's description:

> Sometimes carefully made plans are thrown out of the window in order to respond to one of the fleeting opportunities that classroom life offers ... (Elbaz 1983 p5)

There are two prerequisites for being able to respond 'artistically' to these opportunities. First, the flexibility needed to react to the unforeseen can only come from a broad repertoire of responses available to the teacher. Berliner (1987) points out that experienced teachers' knowledge and skills are, at least partly, a result of the sheer quantity of practice they get throughout their careers. As Bryan and Harter point out in an early study on learning psychology published in 1899:

> Automatism is not genius, but it is the hands and feet of genius. (Bryan and Harter 1899 p375)[1]

Secondly, the 'fleeting opportunities' of the classroom can only be used if they are noticed. It is here that a teacher's perceptions and powers of observation, which were given so much weight in the first three chapters, play a vital role. Schön (1983) reports on an experiment with teachers during which they suddenly recognized a new quality in a student. The teachers had been observing two students on a video recording. The students were engaged in solving a task. One of the students had the wrong solution and the teachers therefore saw him as the less able student. The key moment in the observation occurred when the teachers discovered that it was a trivial error that was at the base of the wrong solution. Moreover, this error had not been his. A new picture of the student now began to emerge. It became clear that he was actually displaying considerable ability in trying to reconcile the contradictions that followed from the initial error. The teachers cast aside preconceptions and arrived at a new perception of the student.

The above example might be seen as an instance of the attitudes described in Chapter 3: the teachers in the end tried to see the student in his own frame of reference and thus saw him as someone unique.

Schön quotes Tolstoy, who describes the art of teaching as seeing each student as an individual with his/her individual difficulties. Teaching considered as an art means having at one's disposal the right method and technique to cope with each individual difficulty and to respond to the uniqueness of such difficulties with unique solutions.

> The best method would be the one which would answer best to all possible difficulties incurred by a pupil, that is, not a method but an art and talent.[2]

Good use of teaching methods means using a method not merely as a technique but being guided by perceptions of students. Such perceptions may be helped by humanistic principles such as empathy, caring and realness. Conversely, method

---

1 I owe this quote to Berliner (1987) in Calderhead (1987).
2 Tolstoy (1967) quoted in Schön (1983) p66.

used sensibly in the classroom is often an indicator for the presence of these principles. Why? Firstly, because those who vary their methods and procedures during a lesson show concern and *care* for the well-being of their classes. Secondly, because they usually look for the right fit between method and group, which means they have both the will and the ability to find out what the state of their class is, thus showing *empathy*. Finally, because it is not only desirable that the method fits the student, but also that it fits the teacher. And this is where the *'realness'* of the teacher (see Chapter 3) comes in. There has traditionally been a lot of research into the efficiency of teaching methods. With hindsight such studies were not very conclusive. Against this background, Stevick has formulated his famous paradox:

> In the field of language teaching, Method A is the logical contradiction of Method B: if the assumptions from which A claims to be derived are correct, then B cannot work, and vice versa. Yet one colleague is getting excellent results with A and another is getting comparable results with B. How is this possible? (Stevick 1976 p104)

Stevick's paradox touches on the realness of the teacher: it is the person who teaches and his/her relationship to the method used that matters. The centrality of the teacher as a person has been pointed out by another author in the field of methodology. Butzkamm (1980), in a summary on the 'bilingual method', stresses the importance of how method and the person of the teacher combine:

> The methods someone uses are part of his everyday behaviour and – admittedly to varying degrees – part of his person. (Butzkamm 1980 p204, my translation)

The credibility of a method and with it, as Stevick's paradox suggests, also its effectiveness, rest on the conviction, credibility and motivation of the person using it. If the right balance between the individuality of the students, the in-dividuality of the teacher, and the discipline imposed by the subject matter is struck, teaching can quite literally become an art:

> ... teaching can be performed with such skill and grace that, for the student as well as for the teacher, the experience can be justifiably characterized as aesthetic. (Eisner 1979 pp175–6)

Trying to capture such moments might well call for new approaches to class-room research. Eisner has argued for new qualitative forms of research. He does not want education to be evaluated entirely in quantitative terms, ie through experiments and with reference to pre-set objectives, but also in a qualitative, personal and artistic way, comparable to the appreciation of art. He calls this kind of evaluation 'connoisseurship'. Interestingly, in advocating it, he moves close to humanistic thought, as humanists (eg Rogers 1985) have argued for a more person-oriented science that takes account of the interplay between the person of the scientist and the discovery – a process described, for instance, in Polanyi (1958). Research on teachers' thinking, like Elbaz's study, can also be seen within this tradition. 'Connoisseurship' may not replace empirical research. It may, however, complement it in a useful way, a point made by Knibbeler (1989 p90). Moreover, the description of teaching as an art may help to redefine the value of teachers' work, not least for teachers themselves. For those practising it, of course, the art of teaching is not only a source of professional esteem but also one of enjoyment. As Connell (1985 p127, his italics) wrote:

> People who have not taught can have little idea of what it is like to have *taught well*.

Epilogue **Year ten**

Diary

21st March

Adults

Did a seminar with parents. An eye-opener. It tells me how moulded I am by my job: I am no longer really used to working with people who are motivated and who want to know something from me. All of a sudden I find myself, in a very polite way, contradicted. I have to retract strongly worded statements about education. Doing so entails no loss of prestige.

20th April

Commitment

Ben in grade 6 wants to read a passage. His reading is rotten. I decide to keep the class waiting and practise one sentence with him until there are no more mistakes in it. He has to read it ten times. The class get mildly interested. Do I want to punish him? He has, after all, volunteered. Exactly for this reason, however, no punishment can be intended. That's how Ben sees the situation, too. He knows that neither the teacher nor the class is against him. There is some laughter, though, when he makes his eleventh attempt. It stops after trial number eleven turns out to be successful.

5th May

Oliver at 26

Met Oliver in the supermarket. Outwardly he hasn't changed much, although he is wearing glasses now. He has, like myself, a baby daughter. Recently he started his own business as a designer. I tell him about the book I am writing. He is amused. At the same time interested. School is over, yet it is never over. We talk about the 'episodes' that happened between us ten years ago. He tells me his sister-in-law is training to be a teacher. He says he feels almost embarrassed thinking about his past as a pupil. They had been a rough lot. Steffen, whose essay I have been keeping so long, is now working on a book himself.

21st June

The flow

It is getting a lesson to flow that makes the difference: one phase merges into the next – at the right moment and with ease. I know what the next phase is, I know how to begin it. I finish saying something and without changing my tone of voice and without any interruption tell the class what to do next.

18th July

On it goes

At times I run out of things to say. Everybody is tired and on it goes: grade 11, grade 7, grade 9, grade 13. I will have to think of something to bring myself and the classes back to life. I must stop drawing out the material just to fill time.

19th July

Harmony in 6d

Routine lessons. We go through some written exercises about tenses. Long columns of verb-forms on the blackboard (Arthur's advice) to which, step by step, more forms are added. If this is the present perfect, what would the past perfect be like? And so on. Very old-fashioned indeed. But both the class and I like it. It is a fixed routine. Everybody knows what they have to do. No discipline problems, because the task carries us through the lesson. I can allow a lot of fun and deviations to happen, because it is easy to get the class back to the task. Everything very relaxed. It is almost like being at home. Tobias tells me so after the lesson.

20th July

Made it up

K retires at the end of the school year. It was his farewell today. He made it up with M. They hadn't been on speaking terms for the last ten years.

26th August

Looking back

Ten years after. Looking back at old diaries, I notice that school is becoming less of a topic to write about. The never-ending drama it used to be ten years ago has gone. More and more I leave the problems at school when I leave school. On the other hand: there are certain things I used to do and that would make the lessons special. These seem to have disappeared with routine. Or they were axed to economize on work, because there is so much marking to do. I have almost forgotten the trouble I once went to in order to make my lessons interesting. I notice when I look at old lesson plans. I am more discerning now: how can aims be reached most economically? The frills have gone. But the frills once made the difference. Pupils were yawning today. I talk too much. When we discuss a text I still find it difficult to focus the talk on a topic, which, despite all the openness I advocate, seems necessary. The questions I asked should have been worked out more carefully.

30th August

A lot of routine these days.

1st September

Splendid lesson in grade 13. Teaching is fun. It can be.

Bibliography

Achtenhagen, F. and Wienold, G. 1975 *Lehren und Lernen im Fremdsprachenunterricht.* Munich: Kösel

Altrichter, H. 1990 *Ist das noch Wissenschaft?* Munich: Profil

Appel, J. 1985 Dolmetschen als Übungsform in der Oberstufe. In *Praxis des neusprachlichen Unterrichts* vol.32, no.1 pp54–8

Appel, J. 1990 Leselust im Unterricht und Unterricht in Leselust. In *Der fremdsprachliche Unterricht* vol.23, no.2 pp39–42

Asher, J. 1969 The TPR-Approach to Language Learning. In *Modern Language Journal* vol.53, no.1 pp3–17

Asher, J. 1977 *Learning another Language through Actions.* Los Gatos, Calif.: Sky Oaks

Ball, S. J. 1980 Initial Encounters in the Classroom and the Process of Establishment. In Woods 1980

Ballantyne, R. M. 1982 (1857) *The Coral Island.* Harmondsworth: Penguin

Bell, J. *et al.* 1985 *Variety: A Workbook for Intermediate Readers.* Cambridge: Cambridge University Press

Berliner, D. C. 1987 Ways of Thinking About Students and Classrooms by More and Less Experienced Teachers. In Calderhead 1987 pp60–83

Bohnsack, F. *et al.* 1984 *Schüleraktiver Unterricht.* Weinheim: Beltz

Brandes, D. and Ginnis, P. 1986 *A Guide to Student-Centred Learning.* Oxford: Blackwell

Brown, G. and Yule, G. 1983 *Teaching the Spoken Language.* Cambridge: Cambridge University Press

Brumfit, C. 1984 *Communicative Methodology in Language Teaching. The Case for Fluency and Accuracy.* Cambridge: Cambridge University Press

Bryan, W. L. and Harter, N. 1899 Studies on the Telegraphic Language. In *The Psychological Review* vol.6, no.4 pp345–75

Buber, M. 1925 Über das Erzieherische. In Buber 1986 (1953) pp11–49

Buber, M. 1986 (1953) *Reden über Erziehung.* Heidelberg: Lambert Schneider

Buber, M. 1955 (1937) *I and Thou.* New York: Scribner

Burghardt, U. 1987 Klage und Antwort im Englischunterricht. Ratschläge für Berufsanfänger. In *Praxis des neusprachlichen Unterrichts* vol.34, no.3 pp262–70

Butzkamm, W. 1980 *Theorie und Praxis der bilingualen Methode.* Heidelberg: Quelle und Meyer

Calderhead, J. 1987 *Exploring Teachers' Thinking.* London: Cassell

Candlin, C. *et al.* 1981 *The Communicative Teaching of English.* London: Longman

Carter, R. and Long, M. 1987 *The Web of Words.* Cambridge: Cambridge University Press

Carr, J. L. 1984 (1972) *The Harpole Report.* Harmondsworth: Penguin

Catford, L. 1979 Portrait of a Ceramics Class. Control and Freedom in a Delicate Balance. In Eisner 1979 pp303–23

Clark, J. L. 1987 *Curriculum Renewal in School Foreign Language Learning.* Oxford: Oxford University Press

Claxton, G. 1989 *Being a Teacher.* London: Cassell

Collie, J. and Slater, S. 1987 *Literature in the Language Classroom.* Cambridge: Cambridge University Press

Connell, R. 1985 *Teachers' Work.* Sydney and London: Allen & Unwin

Cooper, R., Lavery, M. and Rinvolucri, M. 1991 *Video.* Oxford: Oxford University Press

Craik, F. I. M. and Lockhart, R. S. 1972 Levels of Processing: A Framework for Memory Research. In *Journal of Verbal Learning and Behavior* vol.11, no.6 pp671–84

Curran, C. A. 1972 *Counselling–Learning.* New York: Grune and Stratton

Denscombe, M. 1985 *Classroom Control.* London: Allen & Unwin

Doyle, W. 1979 Classroom Effects. In *Theory into Practice* vol.18, no.2 pp138–44

Ehlich, K. 1986 *Muster und Institution.* Tübingen: Narr

Eisner, E. 1979 *The Educational Imagination.* Basingstoke: Macmillan

Elbaz, F. 1983 *Teacher Thinking.* Beckenham: Croom Helm

Ellis, G. and Sinclair, B. 1989 *Learning to Learn English.* Cambridge: Cambridge University Press

Fisch, G. *et al.* 1977 *Learning English. Advanced Modern Practice.* Stuttgart: Klett

Fölsch, G. 1993 Sind "Berufskrankheiten" der Lehrerpersönlichkeit unausweichlich? In *Pädagogik* vol.45, no.1 pp18–22

Francis, P. 1975 *Beyond Control?* London: Allen & Unwin

Frank, C. and Rinvolucri, M. 1983 *Grammar in Action.* Munich: Hueber

Frommer, H. (ed.) 1982 *Handbuch Praxis des Vorbereitungsdienstes. Band 2. Erziehungswissenschaftliche Problemfelder.* Düsseldorf: Schwann Bagel

Goldstein, K. 1940 *Human Nature in the Light of Psychopathology.* Cambridge, Mass.: Harvard University Press

Graef, R. 1990 Lernen durch Lehren. Anfangsunterricht im Fach Französisch. In *Der fremdsprachliche Unterricht* vol.23, no.2 pp10–13

Grell, J. 1974 *Techniken des Lehrerverhaltens.* Weinheim: Beltz

Grellet, F. 1981 *Developing Reading Skills: A Practical Guide to Reading Exercises.* Cambridge: Cambridge University Press

Guiora, A. Z. *et al.* 1975 Language and Person: Studies in Language Behavior. In *Language Learning* vol.25, no.1 pp43–61

Halliday, M. A. K., McIntosh, A. and Strevens, P. 1964 *The Linguistic Sciences and Language Teaching.* London: Longman

Hargreaves, D. H. 1972 *Interpersonal Relations in Education.* London: Routledge & Kegan Paul

Hargreaves, D. H. 1978 What Teaching does to Teachers. In *New Society* vol.43, no.9 pp540–2

Hess-Lüttich, E. W. B. (ed.) 1983 *Textproduktion und Textrezeption.* Tübingen: Narr

Highet, G. 1965 (1951) *The Art of Teaching.* London: Methuen

Hines, B. 1983 *Looks and Smiles.* Harmondsworth: Penguin

Hosenfeld, C. 1976 Learning about Learning. In *Foreign Language Annals* vol.9, no.2 pp117–29

Howatt, A. P. R. 1984 *A History of English Language Teaching.* Oxford: Oxford University Press

Iser, W. 1978 *The Act of Reading: A Theory of Aesthetic Response.* Baltimore: John Hopkins University Press

Johnson, K. and Porter, D. (eds.) 1983 *Perspectives in Communicative Language Teaching*. London: Academic Press

Kiersch, J. (ed.) 1984 *Zum Fremdsprachenunterricht*. Stuttgart: Bund der freien Waldorfschulen

Kirschenbaum, H. and Henderson, V. L. 1990 *The Carl Rogers Reader*. London: Constable

Klyne, P. 1972 *Personenzentrierte Haltungen von Lehrern im Unterricht und ihre Zusammenhänge mit wesentlichen Vorgängen bei älteren Schülern* (PhD dissertation, Hamburg)

Knibbeler, W. 1989 *The Explorative-Creative Way*. Tübingen: Narr

Koch, S. (ed.) 1959 *Psychology: A Study of Science, Vol II*. New York: McGraw-Hill

Kounin, J. S. 1970 *Discipline and Group Management in the Classroom*. New York: Holt, Rinehart and Winston

Krashen, S. 1981 *Second Language Acquisition and Second Language Learning*. Oxford: Pergamon

Krohn, D. 1983 Angst und Englischunterricht. In Solmecke 1983 pp134–76

Labov, W. 1972 The Transformation of Experience in Narrative Syntax. In Labov 1972 pp354–396

Labov, W. 1972 *Language in the Inner City – Studies in Black English Vernacular*. Pittsburgh: University of Pennsylvania Press

Lacey, C. 1977 *The Socialization of Teachers*. London: Methuen

Leeper, R. (ed.) 1967 *Humanising Education*. Alexandria, Virginia: Association for Supervision and Curriculum Development

Legutke, M. 1988 *Lebendiger Englischunterricht*. Bochum: Kamp

Legutke, M. and Thomas, H. 1991 *Process and Experience in the Language Classroom*. London: Longman

Leuschner, G. and Schirmer, F. 1993 Lehrergesundheit aus medizinischer Sicht. In *Pädagogik* vol.45, no.1 pp6–8

Lewin, K. 1935 *A Dynamic Theory of Personality*. New York and London: McGraw-Hill

Littlewood, W. 1981 *Communicative Language Teaching*. Cambridge: Cambridge University Press

Lortie, D. C. 1975 *School-Teacher*. Chicago: Chicago University Press

Maier, M. 1984 Charles Dickens: "A Christmas Carol" in der achten Klasse. In Kiersch 1984 pp121–38

Maley, A. and Duff, A. 1982 (1978) *Drama Techniques in Language Teaching*. Cambridge: Cambridge University Press

Martin, J.-P. 1985 *Zum Aufbau didaktischer Teilkompetenzen beim Schüler auf der lerntheoretischen Basis des Informationsverarbeitungsansatzes*. Tübingen: Narr

Martin, J.-P. 1986 Für eine Übernahme von Lehrfunktionen durch Schüler. In *Praxis des neusprachlichen Unterrichts* vol.33, no.4 pp395–403

Maslow, A. 1987 (1954) *Motivation and Personality*. New York and London: Harper and Row

McDonough, J. 1994 A teacher looks at teachers' diaries. In *English Language Teaching Journal* vol.48, no.1 pp243–52

Morgan, J. and Rinvolucri, M. 1983 *Once upon a Time*. Cambridge: Cambridge University Press

Moskowitz, G. 1978 *Caring and Sharing in the Language Class*. Rawley, Mass.:

Newbury House

Munby, J. 1978 *Communicative Syllabus Design*. Cambridge: Cambridge University Press

Nunan, D. 1989 *Understanding Language Classrooms*. New York: Prentice Hall

O'Neill, R. 1991 The Pausible Myth of Learner-Centredness: or the Importance of Doing Ordinary Things Well. In *English Language Teaching Journal* vol.45, no.4 pp293–304

Polanyi, M. 1958 *Personal Knowledge*. Chicago: Chicago University Press

Prabhu, N. 1987 *Second Language Pedagogy*. Oxford: Oxford University Press

Reichert, E. 1982 Zur Situation des Referendars heute. In Frommer 1982 pp459–85

Reinert, H. 1976 One Picture is Worth a Thousand Words? Not necessarily! In *Modern Language Journal* vol.60, no.4 pp160–7

Reynolds, J. and Saunders, M. 1987 Teacher Responses to Curriculum Policy: Beyond the 'Delivery' Metaphor. In Calderhead 1987 pp195–214

Rinvolucri, M. 1984 *Grammar Games*. Cambridge: Cambridge University Press

Robertson, J. 1989 (1981) *Effective Classroom Control*. London: Hodder and Stoughton

Rogers, C. 1990 (1964) Toward a Modern Approach to Values: The Valuing Process in the Mature Person. In *Journal of Abnormal and Social Psychology* vol.68, no.2 pp160–7 (quoted from Kirschenbaum and Henderson 1990 pp168–85)

Rogers, C. 1990 (1967) The Interpersonal Relationship in the Facilitation of Learning. In Leeper 1967 pp1–18 (quoted in Kirschenbaum and Henderson 1990 pp304–22)

Rogers, C. 1990 (1985) Toward a More Human Science of the Person. In *Journal of Humanistic Psychology* vol.25, no.4 pp7–24 (quoted in Kirschenbaum and Henderson 1990 pp279–295)

Rutter, M. *et al.* 1979 *Fifteen Thousand Hours. Secondary Schools and Their Effects on Children*. London: Open Books

Ryan, K. 1970 *Don't Smile 'till Christmas*. Chicago: Chicago University Press

Sano, M. 1986 How to incorporate Total Physical Response into the English Programme. In *English Language Teaching Journal* vol.40, no.4 pp270–77

Sauer, H. 1985 Sequentialität und Erfolg im Fremdsprachenunterricht. In *Praxis des neusprachlichen Unterrichts* vol.32, no.3 pp282–91

Scheibe, W. 1977 (1969) *Die Reformpädagogische Bewegung: 1900–1932*. Weinheim: Beltz

Schiffler, L. 1989 *Suggestopädie und Superlearning – empirisch geprüft*. Frankfurt: Diesterweg

Schön, D. 1983 *The Reflective Practitioner*. New York: Basic Books

Schön, D. 1990 (1987) *Educating the Reflective Practitioner*. San Francisco: Jossey Bass

Schultze, G. 1993 *Die Erlebnisgesellschaft*. Frankfurt and New York: Campus

Schwerdtfeger, I. C. 1976 *Fremdsprache: mangelhaft*. Paderborn: Schöningh

Sinclair, J. and Coulthard, M. 1975 *Towards an Analysis of Discourse*. Oxford: Oxford University Press

Solmecke, G. (ed.) 1983 *Motivation und Motivieren im Fremdsprachenunterricht*. Paderborn: Schöningh

Spencer, H. 1966 (1859) *On Education and Kindred Subjects*. London: Dent

Everyman's Library

Stein, O. 1989 Wider das Korrigierunwesen. In *Praxis des neusprachlichen Unterrichts* vol.36, no.3 pp265–69

Steiner, R. 1981 (1920) *The Renewal of Education.* Michael Hall: Rudolf Steiner Fellowship Publications

Stevick, E. 1976 *Memory Meaning and Method.* Rawley, Mass.: Newbury House

Stevick, E. 1980 *A Way and Ways.* Rawley, Mass.: Newbury House

Stevick, E. 1990 *Humanism in Language Teaching.* Oxford: Oxford University Press

Thornbury, S. 1991a Watching the Whites of their Eyes: the Use of Teaching-Practice Logs. In *English Language Teaching Journal* vol.45, no.2 pp140–6

Thornbury, S. 1991b Metaphors We Work by. EFL and its Metaphors. In *English Language Teaching Journal* vol.45, no.3 pp193–200

Tolstoy, L. 1967 On Teaching the Rudiments. In Wiener 1967

Turner, B. 1973 *Discipline in Schools.* Ward Lock Educational

van Lier, L. 1988 *The Classroom and the Language Learner.* London: Longman

Wadd, K. 1973 Classroom Power in Discipline in Schools. In Turner 1973

Wadden, P. and McGovern, S. 1991 The Quandary of Negative Class Participation: Coming to terms with Misbehaviour in the Language Classroom. In *English Language Teaching Journal* vol.45, no.2 pp119–127

Wagner, J. 1983 *Kommunikation und Spracherwerb im Fremdsprachenunterricht.* Tübingen: Narr

Warnock, M. 1970 *Existentialism.* Oxford: Oxford University Press

Weinrich, H. 1983a Interview. In *Praxis des neusprachlichen Unterrichts 30* pp44–50

Weinrich, H. 1983b Literatur im Fremdsprachenunterricht – ja, aber mit Phantasie. In Hess-Lüttich 1983 pp11–23

Wesemann, M. 1984 Arbeitplatzstrukturen und unterrichtliche Tätigkeit des Lehrers. In Bohnsack 1984 pp40–120

Whitney, N. 1991 Editorial. In *English Language Teaching Journal 45* p95

Widdowson, H. 1984 The incentive value of theory in teacher education. In *English Language Teaching Journal* vol.38, no.2 pp86–90

Wiener, L. (ed.) 1967 *Tolstoy on Education.* Chicago: University of Chicago Press

Wilkins, D. 1976 *Notional Syllabuses.* Oxford: Oxford University Press

Wilkins, D. 1983 Some issues in Communicative Language Teaching and their Relevance to the Teaching of Languages in Secondary Schools. In Johnson, K. and Porter, D. (eds.) 1983

Woods, P. (ed.) 1980 *Pupil Strategies.* Beckenham: Croom Helm

Zeichner, K. M., Tabachnik, B. R. and Densmore, K. 1987 Individual, Institutional, and Cultural Influences on the Development of Teachers' Craft Knowledge. In Calderhead 1987 pp21–59

Index